5.00

Birds of North America

This book is dedicated to five young Americans,
ERIK, THOMAS, SIBBY, PETER and TIMOTHY
in hopes they will still be able to enjoy
the wildlife described.

Birds of North America

Bertel Bruun

Hamlyn
London · New York · Sydney · Toronto

ACKNOWLEDGEMENTS

Colour

Ardea Photographics – Donald D. Burgess front jacket (top right), front jacket (bottom left), 30 (bottom), 37 (top left), Elizabeth Burgess front jacket (bottom right), 45 (bottom), F. W. Fink 36–37; Trustees of the British Museum (Natural History) 18 (top); Frank V. Blackburn 79 (bottom right); Bruce Coleman Ltd. – Helmut Albrecht 45 (top), Bruce Coleman 18 (bottom), Jack Dermid 37 (top right), James Hancock 36 (top), 90 (top), David Hughes back jacket, Russ Kinne 44 (bottom), 62 (top), Gordon Langsbury 62 (bottom), George Laycock 86–87, Charlie Ott 23 (bottom), 30 (top), 31 (top), 31 (bottom), Ed Park front jacket (top left), 79 (top), Leonard Lee Rue 70 (top), James Simon 79 (bottom left), Joe Van Wormer 22 (top), 63 (right), 70 (bottom); Eric Hosking 23 (top), 91 (right); Jacana – Visage 71; Frank W. Lane – Ronald Austing 63 (left), 90 (bottom), Steve McCutcheon 22 (bottom); Natural History Photographic Agency – James Tallon 78; Bryan Sage 86 (top); Tierbilder Okapia 91 (left); Z.E.F.A. – E. Hummel 19, 44 (top), 87 (top).

Black and white

Ardea Photographics – T. A. Willock 59; Trustees of the British Museum (Natural History) 12; Bruce Coleman Ltd. – Jen and Des Bartlett 49, Jack Dermid 44, Russ Kinne 29, 43, 53, 74, 81, Charlie Ott 15, 34 (top), 64–65, Ed Park 56, Leonard Lee Rue 27, 40, 76, Joe Van Wormer title page, 41, 57, 61, 66–67; David Hosking 48; Eric Hosking 17, 20–21, 24, 26, 33, 46 (bottom), 54, 72, 84–85, Niall Rankin 16, 32, 46 (top), 60; Frank W. Lane – Ronald Austing 34 (bottom), 35, 38, William L. Finley 68, A. Mordan 42, Hugo H. Schroder 28, Lewis W. Walker 69, 75; Janet March-Penney 9; National Audubon Society – John Borneman 82, Allan D. Cruickshank 11; Radio Times Hulton Picture Library 13.

Published by
THE HAMLYN PUBLISHING GROUP LIMITED
London · New York · Sydney · Toronto

Hamlyn House, Feltham, Middlesex, England

Copyright © The Hamlyn Publishing Group Limited 1973

ISBN 0 600 31287 9

Printed in Great Britain

Contents

Foreword

In the days of perfect nature
man lived together with birds and beasts,
and there was no distinction of their kind.
Destruction of the natural integrity
of these things for the production of
articles of various kinds—
this is the fault of the artisan.

Chuang Tzu
369–286 B.C.

The richness of the nature of North America was
immediately recognized by the white men who set eyes
on the land some 450 years ago. But since the arrival of
the settlers, this land has changed with ever increasing
rapidity. Only in recent years have large numbers of the
people inhabiting this continent become aware of the
havoc caused by their activities. Rather feeble attempts
are now being made to save and possibly restore parts of
the past splendor.

This book is an attempt to describe the birds of this
continent as they are today, not as they were before the
white settlers arrived. It is an attempt to show the
changing ecology of North America and its influence on
our birds.

It is my hope this book will help the reader to understand
the importance of conserving our national heritage and
also to gain insight into the changes, beneficial as well
as destructive, that man has forced upon the original
wildlife of the continent.

In writing the book I have received help from my wife,
Ruth, and my secretary, Patricia Williams, to whom I
take the opportunity of extending my gratitude.

Bertel Bruun

The Continent of North America

North America north of the Mexican border with its area of 700,250,000 square miles covers about fifteen per cent of the earth's land area and four per cent of the entire surface of the earth. It is the third largest of the continents.

In the north it is bordered by the almost completely ice-covered Arctic Sea stretching across the North Pole to the forbidding shores of northern Siberia.

In the west the narrow Bering Sea separates North America from the enormous landmass of Asia. Once this sea was dry and animals of many kinds wandered across the land bridge, mixing the faunas of the two worlds. Among these animals were the first men to set foot on the American continent, the American Indians. The Bering Sea opens into the North Pacific, an enormous ocean washing the western shore of North America which through its currents and moisture strongly influences the nature of this area.

To the east the Arctic Ocean blends into the North Atlantic over a wide area. Further south the Hudson Bay opens into the Atlantic, sending its cold currents into the much warmer sea, while even further south the Caribbean, like an enormous bay, separates North America from South America. From here one of the great warm currents of the oceans, the Gulf Stream, enters the Atlantic eventually to expend its enormous amount of energy—stored in the form of heat—on European shores.

The relatively narrow land bridge made by Central America and Mexico forms the western part of the southern boundary. Here the tropical world of South America meets and mixes with the temperate world of North America. In this area a definite natural boundary is difficult to establish, but the Mexican border coincides relatively well with many natural limits which is why it has been chosen for the purpose of this book.

Climatically North America encompasses arctic, temperate and subtropic regions. Along the coasts, particularly the west coast, the neighboring seas moderate the climate and the annual temperature ranges are much less than in the interior.

Both in the east and the west there are mountain chains stretching towards the south. The Rocky Mountains of the west are by far the larger, the Appalachians in the east being pygmy-sized in comparison. Between the two mountain chains the enormous drainage system of the Mississippi River winds south through the central plains.

Geographical and climatic features together determine the nature of the various regions of the North American continent. The plant communities, the basis for all higher life, are most obviously affected by temperature, precipitation and soil condition. These again determine to a large degree the animal life inhabiting them, including the main subject of this work, the birds.

In the north the arctic tundra, the treeless belt bordering the Arctic Sea, stretches across the entire continent. South of it, and similarly reaching from the west to the east coast, is a wide belt of coniferous forest. In the east this is gradually replaced by deciduous woods as one moves south and in the central part by the grasslands of the interior with its once wide-ranging prairies.

Stretching inland from the Pacific coast is a belt of moist coniferous forest containing, among other characteristic trees, the oldest and largest of all living things, the Redwood. In the southwest where the western mountains are spread out over a wider belt than further north, the relatively dry biotic communities of chaparral, sagebrush, pinyon-juniper and desert scrubland are found.

All these regions do not have abrupt borders, but blend into each other, often almost imperceptibly. These transitional zones are known as ecotones.

The coastlines, where the land with its essentially two dimensionally distributed fauna and flora meets the rich tridimensional life of the seas surrounding North America, are very different, for the sea itself has its own characteristic and distinct life in which birds, too, play a role.

The regions described above are idealized regions, communities of nature as they existed before the arrival of man. At the start, when the Indians first settled after their crossing of the Bering Sea land bridge, the change was almost unnoticeable. But soon, even before the arrival of colonizers from the other side of the Atlantic, nature was being changed. Agriculture as practiced by the Indians was changing the land, but its wholesale conversion has taken place only during the last 300 years under the onslaught of western civilization. In many areas the change has been so dramatic it is hard even to imagine what the land looked like before the conversion of ancient natural communities to new high-yielding properties for men whose outlook rarely exceeds that of their own lifespan. In many areas it is sadly difficult to find any remnant of the original natural beauty. So, to the influences on nature of climate and geography we must add the influence of man, an inescapable and prominent part of the continent as it exists today.

If the map of the ecological zones is compared with the one showing the density of population of man on the continent, it will be seen by the description of the birdlife in the various ecological regions that man's greatest influence closely coincides with his numbers in any given area. In addition to these changes, man has created a new habitat, the city, which is described separately in chapter eleven.

In these varied areas of North America about 650 different species of birds find their homes. Each occupies its own ecological niche, a place in nature supplying it with food and shelter. Some spend their entire life within the realms of this single continent, while others are only summer visitors, moving to warmer climates in the cold seasons. It has been estimated that the total bird population at its highest is about twenty billion. Among species this ranges from a mere fifty Whooping Cranes to myriads of the omnipresent Redwings. The distribution of species over the land is extremely varied, from the dense colonies of seabirds with more than one bird per square foot to the virtually birdless salt flats in the northwest of Utah.

In the following sections of this book, the various regions and their birdlife will be explored in greater detail, their looks, habits and relations to other animals, plants and to man.

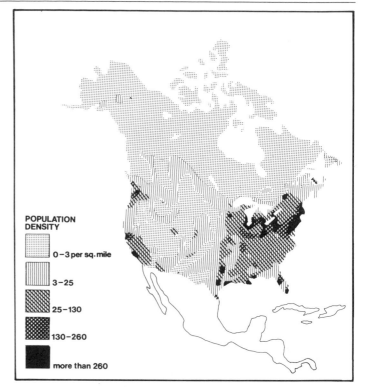

POPULATION DENSITY

☐ 0–3 per sq. mile

▥ 3–25

▨ 25–130

▩ 130–260

■ more than 260

Map of the population density of North America

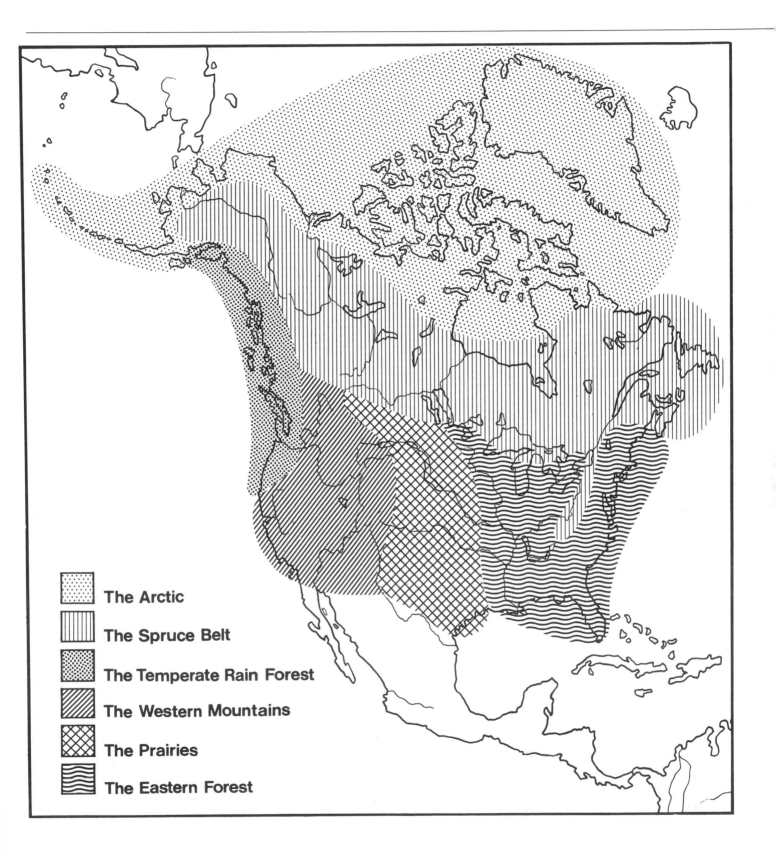

The Arctic

The Spruce Belt

The Temperate Rain Forest

The Western Mountains

The Prairies

The Eastern Forest

Left A combination of mountain, river and conifers characteristic of the southern limit of the spruce belt in the west

The six major ecological regions described in the following chapters; the east and west coasts, as well as the birdlife of the cities, are also described

Man and Birds in North America

The first written record of North American birds comes from the tenth-century Icelandic sagas about the Norsemen crossing from Iceland to Greenland. With regard to birds their descriptions are rather poor, probably because these were species the Norsemen already knew from their home in Iceland. We know, however, they sent Gyrfalcons to the Norwegian king as tribute. In the sagas of the exploration of 'Vinland' only one bird is mentioned by name, the Eider Duck. In Karlsevnis Saga an island Streymoe ('island of strong currents') is mentioned—it was probably what is now known as Belle Isle. Here Eider Ducks nested so close together it was hard to set foot without stepping on either nests or birds. That Eider Ducks should be the one bird mentioned is quite natural as this species played—and plays even today—an important role in the rural economy of Iceland. The downs are widely used for quilts and are harvested on a regular basis. To have an Eider Duck colony on one's land can be likened to a minor gold mine. The Eider Ducks are protected and encouraged to breed so that the downs from the nests can be collected. As the name 'Greenland' was used to lure more settlers to that inhospitable island, so the description of the many Eider Ducks was probably meant as an encouragement for further exploration. But almost 500 years were to elapse, however, before the white man again set eyes on North American birds.

When in the fall of 1492 Columbus made his famous Atlantic crossing, birds were the first signs of the New World he was to discover. On September 18th a large flock of birds was sighted from the *Pinta* and on the following day a Brown Pelican alighted on the *Santa Maria* itself. From then on there were many sightings of birds, several alighting on the ships. Although some were seabirds like the frigatebirds observed on September 29th, others were obviously songbirds on migration. Because of

the many flocks of migrating birds seen flying towards the southwest on October 4th, 5th and 6th, Columbus, in his long search for the rich shores of Asia, decided to change course to follow them. Following this course, on the morning of October 12th he sighted San Salvador and a New World was discovered. From his records, as well as from our knowledge of the migratory habits of North American birds, it is most likely that a large number of the sightings involved Golden Plovers and maybe even the now almost extinct Eskimo Curlew. In the fall these birds leave the coast of eastern Canada and Newfoundland for a direct flight across the ocean,

The white man's first encounters with North American birds

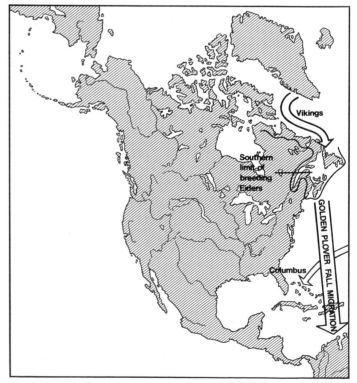

not stopping until the shores of South America have been reached.

Later explorers also mentioned the many birds they saw and particularly remarked upon their abundance. For the early settlers as well as for the Indians originally inhabiting North America birds were important as game, while their feathers and skins were used for decoration and clothing. The Turkey, especially, was an important gamebird.

The first work of importance describing the birds of the New World was *The Natural History of Carolina* by Mark Catesby which appeared in two volumes in the first half of the eighteenth century. Catesby's illustration of the Blue Jay led the naturalist Georg Wilhelm Steller to realize that he had reached North America when on July 20, 1741 he collected a somewhat similar-looking bird at Kayak Island, Alaska. He was a member of an expedition exploring this area for the Russians. This bird has since been named Steller's Jay after its discoverer.

As exploration of this great continent continued, the knowledge of its birds progressed. Among the famous birdwatchers of this early era was William Bartram whose travel journals even today are a delight to read.

In the earliest part of the nineteenth century Alexander Wilson attempted to make a comprehensive illustrated work on the birds of North America. More successful in this respect, however, was John James Audubon whose masterpiece, *The Birds of North America* with its magnificent plates in elephant folio, has a place among the art treasures of the world. Later ornithologists have carried on the proud tradition of Audubon and today the birdlife of North America is one of the best investigated in the world.

Although the first law for the protection of birds—the seasonal protection of game birds in Massachusetts—was enacted before Audubon's work, no less than four species have become extinct (Passenger Pigeon, Carolina Parakeet, Labrador Duck and the Great Auk) and four species must be considered on the verge of extinction (California Condor, Whooping Crane, Eskimo Curlew and Ivory-billed Woodpecker) since that work was completed.

Many more birds, however, would have disappeared from our environment had it not been for the ever increasing efforts made by responsible legislators, individuals and groups of naturalists. A major step in the protection of waterfowl was the passing of the Lacey Act in 1900 which forbade the transportation of illegally acquired game across state boundaries. At that time waterfowl were being shot

in tens of thousands to satisfy the meat markets of the great cities. The Migratory Bird Treaty Act with Canada, which came into effect in 1918 and in 1936 was enlarged to include Mexico, offers protection for all the migratory non-gamebirds and sets up rules for special hunting regulations for migratory gamebirds. The protection of non-migratory birds, however, is left largely to individual states which, in many cases, have been extremely slow in accepting modern concepts of conservation.

Besides the legislation setting up rules for the hunting of various birds, the establishment of national parks, starting with Yellowstone National Park in 1872, has offered sanctuaries for many threatened species, in addition to the National Wildlife Refuge System introduced in 1903. Private organizations like the Audubon Society and the Sierra Club have similarly played a most important role in the protection of birds and other wildlife. Thus it is largely due to the efforts of the Audubon

The Whooping Crane is still close to extinction despite the conservation efforts on its behalf; it has now been bred successfully in captivity in an attempt to build up a 'reserve stock'

Society that the American and Snowy Egrets, once hunted for the use of their feathers in the millinery industry, have survived and are now able to thrive again in North America. This and other successes have been made possible by a combination of sanctuaries and education of the public. With the ever increasing urbanization of our society, such a policy is essential for the survival of at least token examples of the fauna and flora of the great North American continent.

It may be worthwhile to dwell a little on the species which have disappeared for ever and on the causes of their tragic fate.

The Great Auk, a large seabird which, like the penguin of the Southern Hemisphere, had lost its ability to fly, once nested in abundance on Funk Island and possibly other islands off Newfoundland. Here it found refuge from landbound predators. But as the white man extended his world to the North Atlantic coast of North America, the fate of this northern 'penguin' was sealed. Fishermen harvesting a rich catch from the sea on the Newfoundland banks found the Great Auk an easy prey; its meat was a welcome supplement to their diet and a useful bait for the fishhook. Later, local inhabitants also pursued the bird for its feathers. By the early part of the nineteenth century it had disappeared from North American waters and the last specimens were taken off Iceland on June 3rd, 1844.

The Labrador Duck, originally nesting in the northeastern part of North America, was a sea duck, not dissimilar to the Common Eider Duck. It was hunted on its wintering grounds off the eastern coast, and the last one recorded was from Elmira, N.Y. on December 12th, 1878. As hunting on the wintering grounds can scarcely have been the cause of its extinction, it is more likely that the wholesale destruction of wildfowl further north was the main cause of its disappearance, as it was of the extinction of the Great Auk.

The Carolina Parakeet was once very common along the eastern seaboard, where it was relentlessly hunted for the damage it was said to do to fruits and

The Great Auk, here depicted by Audubon, became extinct in 1814

White-headed Eagle. FALCO LEUCOCEPHALUS, Linn. Male. Yellow Catfish

crops. Furthermore, this social bird had the habit of hovering over wounded companions shot to the ground, making the task of the hunter very easy. The ever increasing pressure of man on its last stronghold in the wild cypress swamps of the southeast finally brought it to extinction, the last verified record of the species being from 1904 when it was found in Florida.

Even more spectacular was the sudden disappearance of the Passenger Pigeon. This pigeon was once one of the most numerous of all North American birds. It was extremely social in habits, flocks numbering hundreds of thousands and even millions of birds. These swarms naturally caused damage to crops and were hunted with every conceivable weapon, even canister-loaded cannons. Its rapid downfall in the latter part of the last century, when a mere twenty years saw the disappearance of all its multitudes, was aided by the fact that the bird was so social in its nesting habits that successful breeding required the stimulus of thousands of others of

Audubon called the Bald Eagle, the national bird of the United States, the White-headed Eagle

its kind engaged in the same activity. The last Passenger Pigeon died in the Cincinnati Zoo in 1914.

These examples should suffice to demonstrate that the naturalist has to be on a constant alert to avoid similar tragedies occurring in the future. Even the national symbol of the United States, the Bald Eagle, is thus endangered.

The Bald Eagle was chosen for the American national emblem in 1782 despite the protestations of Benjamin Franklin who preferred the wild Turkey. Once ranging over almost the entire continent of North America, it is now limited to a few strongholds, particularly Alaska and Florida. However, it has been continually decreasing in numbers at a rate of about ten to fifteen per cent per decade since DDT and other insecticides toxic to vertebrates have been used widely. Its future survival is seriously threatened and major efforts may be required to save it.

The Arctic

Arctic North America stretches all the way from Alaska to Greenland. Geographically it is best defined as the area which is found north of the tree line, the land which is so cold that trees cannot survive. The boundary with the broad belt of coniferous forests found south of it, however, is not sharp; islands of woods are found in the arctic tundra and areas of tundra interrupt the shadowy forests.

The climatic conditions of the arctic are extremely adverse as the summers, although pleasant, are so short that the deeper layers of the ground remain frozen. Although the landscape ranges through tundra, forest tundra, mountains, deserts, islands and lakes, the climate unites these different habitats into a fairly well-defined zone. Most parts of the arctic are found north of the Arctic Circle and therefore enjoy midnight sun during the summer. During this season, many areas supply a lush community of plants and insects which is the basis of life for tens of thousands of birds which travel hundreds, or even thousands of miles each year to take advantage of this short-lasting, but extremely abundant, food supply.

Only a few hardy species remain during the cold arctic winter. During this long period the days are short with a low-set sun, although the nights may be bright with the illumination of spectacular bursts of Northern Lights. The land birds must search for food hidden beneath the snow or on the windswept mountain slopes. Only here and there do bushes and branches stick up above the surface, offering a few buds to be picked by the hardy sparrow-like Hornemann's Redpoll and Snow Buntings, or the more resourceful ptarmigans which can also dig through the snow to find not only food but shelter from the forbiddingly cold winds above. Two kinds of ptarmigans, the northern Rock Ptarmigan and the Willow Ptarmigan, inhabit the arctic. In summer they are both speckled brown and white, blending well into the tundra vegetation, but in winter they are white, giving them at least partial protection against the Snowy Owls and Gyrfalcons which prey upon them.

The Raven, almost cosmopolitan in its distribution, is also found here in the far north. Never rejecting the slightest morsel of food, it is able to manage through the winter. Like the Snow Bunting, it often takes advantage of scraps left by the few humans living in this bleak region; both birds are often found near Eskimo villages which offer them better opportunities of finding food than the barren tundra.

But as the days lengthen, the snow starts to melt, the frozen barren ground turns into a vast field crisscrossed by streams and dotted with thousands of lakes and ponds. In June and July myriads of birds arrive to raise a new generation of their species.

Most of the sandpipers known as 'Peeps' nest here—Baird's, Semi-palmated, Least, Pectoral, and White-rumped Sandpipers and Dunlin spread out over the tundra. Knots find their refuge in the mountains and along the shores Purple Sandpipers and Sanderlings are found in great numbers. Other shore birds also find their homes in the tundra; for example, Golden Plovers with their plaintive whistle are common, while Hudsonian Godwits and Whimbrels with their curved bills have more restricted ranges. Stilt Sandpipers and Yellowlegs wade in the shallow ponds, a habitat they share with Northern or Red-necked Phalaropes. Phalaropes—particularly the two arctic species, the Northern and the Red or Gray Phalarope—are very good swimmers. They spend the winters far out to sea where they live on zoo-plankton, while in summer the arctic ponds supply them with an abundance of food. Often they are seen swimming in small circles to stir up the bottom water and bring to the surface food items otherwise inaccessible to them. The female phalaropes are the more brightly colored and it is they that initiate the courtship. After they have laid their eggs, the males take over the incubation and also care for the young when they are hatched.

Ducks are common in the arctic. Pintails and Old-squaws or Long-tailed Ducks as well as Surf Scoters, Common Scoters and White-winged Scoters are found nesting on lake shores, although in winter the latter four at least are typical seabirds. They share the lakes with the four species of loons—or divers as they are known in Europe: Common or Great Northern, Yellow-billed, Arctic and Red-throated, all of which also retire to seashores for the winter. Eider Ducks nest along the seashores and the more northerly distributed King Eider nests in colonies on small islands offshore. But more spectacular than the ducks are the skeins of Snow Geese which every spring fly north in large flocks to inhabit this arctic territory. On migration they follow well-established ancient routes as they return from their wintering grounds on the mid-Atlantic shore, the Mississippi Delta and the west coast. The very similar, but much smaller, Ross's Goose has a very restricted breeding range in the Perry River region and migrates over a narrow front to its wintering grounds in the central valley of California. Also primarily western in distribution is the White-fronted Goose which only rarely winters east of the Mississippi River.

The Brant or Brent Goose breeds in the eastern part of the arctic. It is a small goose, only about half the size of the average Canada Goose. It is found on both sides of the Atlantic. In winter Brants live to a large degree on the eel grass which is abundant in bays and offshore along the Atlantic coasts. In the early 1930s these enormous 'plains' of eel grass were devastated by disease, causing a precipitous drop in the number of Brants. However, the eel grass has slowly regained its former abundance and Brants are once more a common sight along the shores of the Atlantic. In spite of his once intensive hunting of Brants, man played only a minor role in this disaster. The protection of the goose would have done little had it not been for the recuperative powers of the seaweed—an example of the delicate balance of nature, with its wide-ranging inter-

The Willow Ptarmigan is one of the few birds able to withstand the rigors of the arctic winter

dependence on many forms of life. The Black Brant, the western counterpart of the Brant, fared better; as its food resources were spared the blight, its population has remained relatively stable.

The many birds in the north are preyed upon by a number of predatory species. Snowy Owls, Gyrfalcons, Peregrine Falcons and Golden Eagles take their toll of the larger birds. The Peregrine Falcon, once common and widespread over most of the continent, actually finds the arctic its last stronghold. Persecution by man and the reclamation of wild land have both had their share in causing the slow decline of this species. In the late 1950s and 1960s, however, a catastrophic fall in population

Left Brants nest in the arctic. They spend the winter on the seashore

Below The cosmopolitan Peregrine Falcon has found one of its last strongholds in the arctic

took place which threatened this majestic bird with extinction. The cause was the irresponsible large-scale use of insecticides in the United States. Along with other predators, this species is now seriously threatened by the slow but unintended poisoning. It is ironic that man, who for centuries has waged a merciless, although only partially successful, campaign against what he erroneously considered vermin but is at last beginning to understand the true place of the predators in nature, has now hit upon and unleashed a weapon more powerful than thousands of guns and traps. The unanswered question is whether we are able to reverse this process of the destruction of our environment by insidious poisoning.

The Rough-legged Hawk, the Short-eared Owl and the Long-tailed and Pomarine Jaegers, or Skuas as they are known in the Old World, also prey upon lemmings and other rodents. The two jaegers are

Right The illustration of the Blue Jay in Catesby's book which made Steller realize he had reached the New World

Below The Snowy Egret was saved largely owing to the efforts of the Audubon Society

Opposite Steller's Jay is named after Georg Wilhelm Steller who first saw it in Alaska

closely related to the gulls and in winter spend their time on the high seas. Like their close relative, the Parasitic Jaeger or Arctic Skua, they do not refrain from robbing other seabirds of their catch.

The fluctuation in numbers of rodents, with peak populations every four years, paired with the slower fluctuations of ptarmigans, which peak every ten years, strongly influences the food resources of their predators. Breeding success is great in years of abundance, but these are followed by summers of scarce resources, often causing such species as Snowy Owls to emigrate far south of their normal range.

Many cliffs on arctic shores are teeming with life as numerous seabirds seek their nesting grounds here close to the abundant food supply offshore. On the cliffs they find relative safety on the ledges which foxes and other predators cannot reach. Most cliffs where seabird colonies are found not only have a large number of individuals, but also a fair number of different species. Razorbills and Black Guillemots hide their nests among the rocky boulders where the sea pounds the shore. The Great Cormorant in the east and the Pelagic Cormorant in the west have more exposed nests. Above them on the narrow ledges of the vertical cliff murres or guillemots lay their single egg, while Kittiwake nests cling to the slightest irregularity on the cliff surface. Puffins nest at the bottom of intricate tunnels they dig in the

Semi-diagrammatic representation of the typical nesting sites of cliff-nesting birds of the North Atlantic

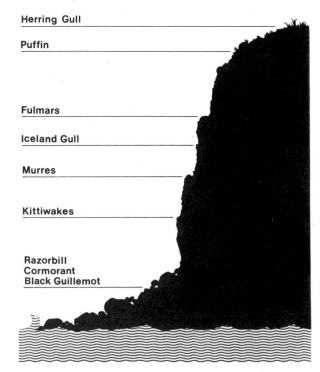

Herring Gull

Puffin

Fulmars

Iceland Gull

Murres

Kittiwakes

Razorbill
Cormorant
Black Guillemot

The Parasitic Jaeger occurs in a light color phase as well as in a uniformly dark phase

Right Wilson's Snipe makes its home in the many bogs on the tundra

Below The breeding cycle of the Lesser Snow Goose is closely adapted to the short arctic summers

Opposite Snow Buntings arrive in their northern breeding grounds before the snow is off the ground

Opposite inset Snowy Owls may in certain years travel far south of the arctic

grassy slopes above. Other inhabitants of these often enormous seabird colonies are Glaucous, Iceland and Herring Gulls, which frequently take a toll of the eggs and young of their neighbors.

In the high arctic there are colonies of hundreds of thousands of Little Auks. Along the Bering Sea Horned and Tufted Puffins, auklets and murrelets form colonies beside the murres or guillemots.

On some islands off southeastern Canada there are colonies where the stately Gannet nests in thousands.

The basis for these concentrations of seabirds is the richness of the sea offshore where cold and warm currents meet and mix. This fertile combination supports an enormously rich life of plankton, preyed upon by both fish and birds.

Gulls are common in the arctic, including such species as Herring, Ivory, Glaucous, Iceland and Sabine's Gulls. Although their breeding ranges overlap in several places, their different feeding habits preclude inter-specific competition.

The nesting ground of the greatest traveler of all birds, the Arctic Tern, is also in the arctic. Nesting in colonies these birds take advantage of the midnight sun, but when the short summer is over they take off on a transoceanic journey which brings them to the Antarctic waters so rich in the small marine life on which the species thrives. Here, during the summer of the Southern Hemisphere, they again enjoy the long hours of daylight.

In western Alaska, as well as eastern Greenland, there are species of birds which have invaded the arctic from the Old World, to which they retreat in winter. Such species as Arctic Warbler and Yellow Wagtail are found in Alaska, whereas eastern Greenland is the breeding ground for Barnacle and Pink-footed Geese.

Arctic Terns, which nest in the far north and winter near Antarctica, are the greatest travelers of all birds

The Spruce Belt

South of the arctic, a wide belt of trees dominated by coniferous species—the spruce belt—stretches from the coast of Alaska through the entire continent to the Gulf of St Lawrence. Characteristic of this forest, especially in the west, are thousands of lakes and ponds and a multitude of rivers and streams. Over 1,000 miles in width, this belt is the largest ecological zone in North America.

The northern half of the spruce belt consists of quite open woods gradually blending into the arctic tundra. Here the trees are stunted in growth and scattered groups of trees alternate with open bogs mainly covered with moss ('muskeg'). South of this semi-open landscape, however, the trees become taller and the forest denser, finally becoming an almost impenetrable wilderness of spruce, firs, pines and other northern trees. In the west the southern limit of this enormous forest is the northern part of the magnificent Rocky Mountains. Further east the spruce belt is separated from the northern prairies by a very narrow belt of deciduous forest. In the region of the Great Lakes, the spruce belt dips below the United States' border where it meets the great eastern deciduous forest. Here, and all the way to the Atlantic, the two types of forest intermix.

In the Appalachians many areas are covered with stands of evergreens, the higher altitudes setting these areas apart from the surrounding deciduous forest. This southern, almost tail-like, extension of dense evergreen forest is reflected in the distribution of many species of birds characteristic of the spruce belt. One example is the Slate-colored Junco, the breeding distribution of which is shown in the diagram on this page. This handsome little black and white bird which winters practically throughout the United States is found nesting almost exclusively in, but throughout, the spruce belt.

Except in the east, this vast ecological zone is relatively undisturbed by man. Increasing lumbering activities, however, are a rising threat to this almost unimaginably large and rich forest. Together with the arctic, it is the only large area of true wilderness in North America.

The birdlife of the spruce belt is very rich and varied. The open areas of the north are the breeding grounds for several shorebirds, the lakes harbor multitudes of ducks in the summer and the forest itself is teeming with songbirds.

In the early summer the yodel-like call of the Common Loon or Diver is a familiar sound of the northern forest. The Common Loon, which in summer plumage has two bands of white spots like necklaces on its black neck, is a large fish-eating

The breeding range of the Slate-colored Junco. The map shows its striking correspondence with the spruce belt

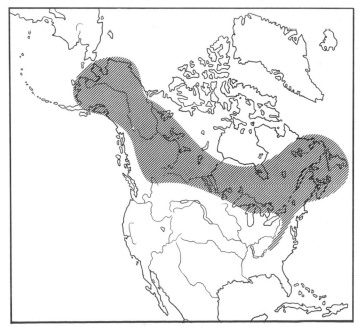

waterbird with short pointed wings and webbed feet. It nests at the edge of the deep clear lakes where it catches fish of many sorts. In winter it migrates to the sea coast. Its plumage is then much more somber, battleship-gray above, white below. Two grebes also live in the western lakes. The larger of the two, the Red-necked Grebe, nests singly, whereas the Horned Grebe often nests in colonies. They both prefer less open lakes than the Common Loon. This is also true of the Pied-billed Grebe which replaces them in the east. They spend the winter along the coasts, the Horned Grebe often in loose flocks close by the shore.

On islands in some of the Great Lakes north of the prairies there are colonies of White Pelicans. They prefer shallow lakes and obtain their food by scooping up fish and tadpoles with their enormous bills. They frequently feed in flocks, sometimes spreading out in a long line and chasing shoals of fish towards the shallow waters of the shoreline where they are easier to catch. Often the White Pelicans share these fish-rich waters with the Double-crested Cormorant, the only species of cormorant reaching this far inland.

But more than anything else, the ducks dominate the life on the lakes of the spruce forest. Literally millions each summer find nesting sites, especially in the northwest. In the east only relatively few species—Black Ducks, Common Goldeneyes and Ring-necked Ducks—are common, although species such as the Baldpate Teal or American Wigeon, Blue-winged and Green-winged Teal and even Redhead and Canvasback have recently increased in numbers in the east. In the northwest, however, all

Horned Grebes build floating nests among reeds

these species are much more common and numerous together with Pintail, Shoveler, Mallard, Greater and Lesser Scaup, Bufflehead, Ruddy Duck, White-winged and Surf Scoters. Each species has its own preference for a particular type of lake or pond but each is able to find a suitable habitat in this enormous wilderness. In the fast-moving streams of the westernmost area, Barrow's Goldeneye and Harlequin Duck, both spectacular birds to encounter, find their summer homes.

Mergansers are diving ducks with narrow, serrated bills for catching fish. All three North American species, Common Merganser or Goosander, Red-breasted and Hooded Mergansers, inhabit this region. Both Common and Hooded Mergansers nest

in tree cavities as the Common Goldeneye does. When eggs are hatched the ducklings jump to the ground and follow their mother in an overland march to the nearest lake. This is probably the most dangerous walk these birds make in their lives as they easily fall prey to predators of all kinds—particularly racoons, weasels and hawks. Once in the water, however, they can avoid many of these dangers by their ability to dive expertly.

Canada Geese are common throughout the spruce belt, often in large numbers. Other geese, however, are more northern in their distribution.

The Trumpeter Swan, heaviest of all waterfowl with its weight of up to thirty pounds, was once common here as well as in the northern prairie lakes. Relentlessly hunted and relatively tame, this magnificent bird was headed towards rapid extinction until the first half of this century when efforts to conserve

A Common Goldeneye duckling seeks refuge under its mother

it were undertaken. This was done primarily in Yellowstone National Park. The success here has been so great that birds are now 'exported' and reintroduced on lakes where the species formerly bred. Although still rare, it has been saved and is increasing in numbers in its originally wide area of distribution in the northwest. Its present status is an example of the kind of successful wildlife management which is so essential for the survival of many of our birds.

Less successful, although more publicized, have been the efforts to conserve the stately Whooping Crane. Although probably never numerous, the species was once found breeding through large parts of central North America. Hunting and agriculture soon destroyed its breeding grounds in the southern part of the continent and by the early part of this century the total population had dwindled to less than 100. By 1940 only a couple of dozen birds were left. These wintered along the Gulf coast where

in 1937 the Aransas National Wildlife Refuge was established specifically for the protection of the wintering Whooping Cranes. Their nesting grounds were unknown till 1954 when they were discovered in the extensive bogs of Wood Buffalo Park in the Northwest Territory. Since then the Whooping Crane has successfully bred in captivity. This has been done in an attempt to build up a 'reserve stock' should a natural disaster of some kind overcome the remaining small wild flock.

Conservation efforts also include newspaper campaigns at the time of migration in the area traversed by these spectacular white birds to protect them from accidental shooting. But even with these efforts

Right This Downy Woodpecker has been attracted to a mixture of suet and seeds

Below The thousands of Canada Geese nesting in the lakes congregate in large flocks in winter

Below A displaying Spruce Grouse is one of the most
spectacular sights of the northern forest

Bottom Cedar Waxwings to a large degree live on berries

Right Trumpeter Swans, the largest waterfowl in the world, were close to extinction but are now increasing in numbers

Below The yodeling call of the Common Loon is a characteristic sound on the northern lakes

the total population today is only about fifty, far from the level where it can be considered 'saved'.

Along the shores of the lakes, particularly in the northern part of the spruce belt, several shorebirds nest. Solitary Sandpiper and both Yellowlegs—the Greater and Lesser—breed here. The two Yellowlegs are best told apart by their calls, the Lesser having a short one to three note whistle, the Greater a longer three to five note whistle. The dumpy Short-billed Dowitcher also nests here as does the Common Snipe, the courtship flight of which is commonly seen and heard over the boggy marshes. It gives a characteristic buzzing sound, produced by the vibration of its tail feathers, as it swoops down in an impressive dive. The Upland Plover nests in dry open areas and the Spotted Sandpiper along streams and lakes.

In marshes with dense vegetation Sora and Yellow Rail share their elusive habits with the Bittern, the only representative of the heron family found this far north.

Several species of gull are common, especially by the larger lakes and swamps. Herring, California, Ring-billed, Franklin's and Bonaparte's Gulls are all common breeding birds. In recent years the Little Gull of Old World origin has been found nesting in very small numbers. It is still uncertain if this charming species, which spends the winter at sea, will be able to establish itself in the New World.

The birdlife in the dense forest is very different from that found in the open. One of the most characteristic birds of this forest is the Spruce Grouse, also called the 'fool hen' because of its tameness. This gamebird survives the winter on a diet of conifer needles and the buds of evergreens. In spring the male selects a display ground in a small clearing and tries to attract females by the whirring of its wings and strutting display. The Ruffed Grouse is also common, although it usually prefers less dense forest with more clearings and lower vegetation. Its display consists of a peacock-like fanning of the tail and a far-carrying 'drumming' produced by vigorous wing flapping. Another inhabitant of the wood also produces sounds with its wings. This is the Common Nighthawk which can be found throughout most of North America. At dusk the humming buzz of the wing is a common sound as the bird dives in its display.

Several woodpeckers are common. The Yellow-bellied Sapsucker drills rows of holes in the trees, returning later to feed on the sap that has oozed out and the insects which this has attracted. Black-backed and Northern Three-toed Woodpeckers are residents of these forests as are much more wide-spread Hairy and Downy Woodpeckers. The Yellow-shafted Flicker, however, dependent as it is on ants found on the ground, migrates to the eastern United States for the winter.

Songbirds of many kinds are numerous. Olive-sided, Yellow-bellied, Least and Traill's or Alder Flycatchers are each common in their preferred habitats, but more dominant are the many warblers found in these woods. They fill many of the niches the forest supplies, each species having its own preferred habitat for which it is best equipped to compete with other species. Living on insects, they all have to move south in winter, many of these small birds traveling the thousands of miles to the tropical lushness of South America. Some of the most common and widespread are the Tennessee, Magnolia, Cape May, Myrtle, Blackpoll, Bay-breasted, and Palm Warblers. It will be noted that many seem inappropriately named from plants and places not even near the Canadian forest. This is because they were first encountered and described on their migration through the eastern colonies. The names of these birds, whose nesting grounds were unknown to the colonists, are not very helpful—and often downright confusing—for the novice bird-watcher.

Thrushes are common in this forest. Swainson's and Gray-cheeked Thrushes, Veery and Robin all inhabit this area and, like the warblers, are migratory.

Seed-eating species also abound. White-winged

Right A male Red Crossbill feeds its incubating mate

Below Traill's or Alder Flycatchers are common in swamps

or Two-barred and Red Crossbills live on the seeds of evergreens and therefore do not have to migrate. As their food supply fluctuates, however, they may in certain years invade other areas where they are not normally found. Crossbills often nest very early in the spring when the weather is still cold and snow covers the trees. The eggs, even the newly hatched young, cannot be left unprotected for even a few minutes or they would freeze to death and are therefore brooded constantly. Pine Siskins, Evening Grosbeaks, Slate-colored Juncos, Savannah, Tree, White-throated and Song Sparrows are seed-eating birds which have to travel southward in winter to survive, like the fruit-eating Bohemian and Cedar Waxwings.

On this mass of birds others prey. Nest and eggs are constantly robbed by Common Crows, Gray and Blue Jays, and the Raven is common throughout the area. This enormous crow-like bird lives on a very varied diet, but prefers carcasses and small or wounded animals which it can easily overcome.

Goshawks and Sharp-shinned Hawks are specialized in pursuit of birds in the forest. Marsh Hawks or Hen Harriers and Red-tailed Hawks live mainly on rodents and like the Pigeon Hawk or Merlin, which is really a small falcon, they prefer more open terrain. Owls, such as the Great Horned, Long-eared and Short-eared, Hawk and Boreal species are common, mainly preying on rodents of the forest floor.

Above Gray Jays often frequent campsites in their search for food

Below Red-tailed Hawks will defend their nests against any intruder

34

The Eastern Forest

Stretching south from the eastern end of the coniferous forest belt of Canada is an enormous area, once almost completely covered with woods. These woods of deciduous trees of many varieties were interspersed with smaller or larger stands of spruce and pine, particularly in the mountains. In the south they gave way to the southern pine forest and large swamps with magnificent stands of cypress. West of the Alleghenies open parkland dominated the landscape as it slowly blended into the western prairie.

More than any region in North America this area has been changed by man. It was here that the European settlers along the eastern seaboard first cleared the land for farms. As the pressure of population rose, the movement west gathered impetus and more and more trees were felled and forests cleared to give way to fields and meadows. Once the mountain barrier was passed, the most fertile parkland was brought under the plow. The earth was found to be not only fertile but also rich in minerals, and today this western half of the region is a vast agricultural plain intermixed with large industrial complexes. The original parkland still exists, but only in patches. Further east many of the old farms were later abandoned, however, and the forest again reclaimed much of its territory.

The mountains themselves, always marginal land in regard to farming, have been left more undisturbed.

The southern part of the east is largely flats covered by pine forest. This is a large area interspersed with farmland and in other areas with swamps.

The peninsula of Florida juts out in the southeastern corner of this region. This state with its prairies, swamps, and the Everglades formed by a very wide, shallow and slow-flowing river, in many respects differs from other areas in North America. In addition there are extensive mangrove swamps on many of the coasts of Florida.

In spite of the great changes in the landscape most of the birds, particularly the smaller ones, can still be found either in the 'islands' of virgin land or in the man-made habitats resembling their natural surroundings. Hedgerows in farmland, and gardens and parks in and around cities in many ways resemble the clearings or more open parts of the forest. The fields have benefited the grassland species and, as the abandoned farms are reclaimed, scrubland birds move in.

Although small in size, warblers form an important element in the avifauna of this region. With the exception of the open farmland almost every type of forest and parkland has its characteristic species exploiting the ecological niches. As warblers are insect-eaters, most are present only in the summer

The Kentucky Warbler is a characteristic bird of the rich moist woodlands of the east

Right The brilliance of the Cardinal makes it one of the most attractive of North American birds

Centre Baltimore Orioles make large pendular nests, intricately woven together

Far right The Indigo Bunting is a common and attractive inhabitant of the farmland which replaced the forest in the east

Bottom The Little Blue Heron stalks its prey in ponds and swamps

months, in the fall performing a nocturnal mass exodus to more hospitable climates in the south.

In the mature deciduous forest Black-and-white Warblers are seen feeding along the trunks and large branches. In the canopy Black-throated Green Warblers and Blackburnian Warblers explore the leaves for insects of various kinds. On the forest floor the Ovenbird, a thrush-like warbler with a spotted breast, builds its domed nest. Its song, often rendered as 'tea-cher', is one of the characteristic sounds of the woods. Many varieties of warblers find their niches in damp woods and swamps. Parula, Cerulian and Hooded Warblers make their homes high in the trees. Nearer the undergrowth Kentucky Warblers are found and the American Redstart, forever flicking its colorful tail, restlessly pursues flying insects. Along the streams the Louisiana Waterthrush can be found and, if lucky, it is also possible in these moist forests to encounter one of the rarest of North American birds, Bachman's Warbler. Where evergreens exist Black-throated Blue Warbler, Yellow-throated Warbler and Pine Warbler can be seen. In the shrubbery and thickets, which man's use of the land has made so abundant, the birdwatcher will find the Yellow Warbler, the most widespread of all North American Warblers; it probably reaches its greatest abundance in this region. The Chestnut-sided Warbler is another species to which the changing of the landscape has been a great advantage. The Yellow-throat and the Yellow-breasted Chat, both transcontinental species, exploit the same habitat.

In the areas where forest is reclaiming land the Golden-winged Warbler and the closely related

Blue-winged Warbler can be found among the young trees. Where the ranges of these two species overlap they sometimes interbreed, giving rise to hybrid forms—to the perplexity of the birdwatcher encountering them. The Nashville Warbler and the misnamed Prairie Warbler also live in this habitat.

In this connection the rarest of North American warblers, Kirtland's Warbler, deserves mention. This species is found only in the northernmost part of Michigan where it nests in tracts of medium-sized jackpines. Its nesting habits are so specialized it cannot use any other habitat or type of tree. The area where it nests is managed by occasional burning, keeping the jackpines at the right age. Even with this extensive management, however, the species has not increased, but on the contrary is probably now decreasing in numbers, the total population being only a couple of hundred. At the present time it appears that the gravest danger for this species is the fact that it is strongly parasitized by cowbirds.

Another group of songbirds common in the eastern deciduous forest region are the vireos. Vireos are much less brilliantly colored than the warblers and not as lively. Although, like warblers, they are insectivores, their bills are heavier. The Red-eyed Vireo is the most abundant of all the songbirds of the deciduous forest. Its beautiful Robin-like song can be heard in almost every patch of wood. Much rarer are the White-eyed Vireo, which prefers dense thickets, and the Yellow-throated Vireo, which is found in parkland with open shade trees. The Warbling Vireo is difficult to see as it prefers the canopies of tall trees where its nest is found hanging in a fork high above the ground.

Black-capped Chickadees and the very similar Carolina Chickadees are two other small songbirds which are common in the forest, as is their relative, the Tufted Titmouse. All three, as well as the White-breasted Nuthatch, are easily attracted to birdfeeders, particularly in gardens near patches of woodland.

The Ruby-throated Hummingbird is the only member of its family found in the east. It is a summer visitor only as it depends on flowering plants for its food. In habits it closely resembles the many different hummingbirds found in the west.

Thrushes are characteristic woodland birds.

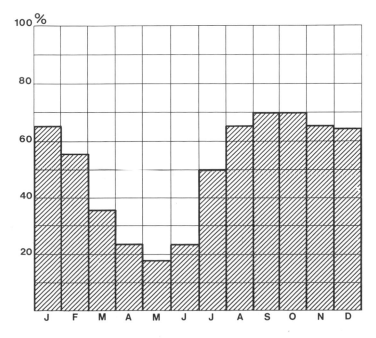

Far left The Prairie Warbler is misnamed – it does not occur on the prairie but in deciduous saplings

Left Graph showing percentage of plant food eaten by the Robin throughout the year. Animal food is mainly eaten in the spring, fruits and seeds in other seasons

Besides the ubiquitous Robin, which, as other members of its family, lives on a mixed diet, two species inhabit the eastern deciduous forest. One is the Wood Thrush, often seen searching the forest floor for snails, worms and insects, while the other, the Veery with its rust-colored back, prefers to seek its food near streams or ponds. Catbirds are also numerous in woods, particularly where there is dense cover. The Brown Thrasher, too, is common. More brilliantly colored birds to be encountered are the orange and black Baltimore Oriole, the bright red Scarlet Tanager and the Rose-breasted Grosbeak. All three are common inhabitants of tall and mature forests.

Woodpeckers, whose drumming on the trees can be heard throughout the summer, are represented by both the Hairy and the Downy Woodpeckers. The Yellow-shafted Flicker, which often seeks its food on the ground, particularly on anthills, is common.

The large family of flycatchers is also represented in the forest. The Great Crested Flycatcher, famed for ornamenting its nest with snakeskins, and the small and inconspicuous Acadian Flycatcher and Eastern Wood Pewee are all found in this habitat.

The birds of prey, once commonly seen throughout the area, are getting scarce. The typical woodland species are Cooper's Hawk and Sharp-shinned Hawk, both of which in their darting flight are able to pick up unsuspecting warblers or other small birds for food. The Red-tailed, Red-shouldered, and Broad-winged Hawks all find their nesting sites in the woods, but to a large degree live upon rodents which they find in nearby fields. They are often seen soaring high above the trees in apparently never ending circles. At night the Great Horned Owl and the Screech Owl take over the hunting of prey.

As the northern forest blends into the pine barrens of the south, species characteristic of this area are added to the avifauna. Such species are Brown-headed Nuthatch, Summer Tanager and Red-cockaded Woodpecker. Others become more common, like the Pileated Woodpecker which, however, can be encountered as far north as Canada.

The farmland of the east is inhabited by many species of birds. Some, such as the sparrow-like Dickcissel, were originally prairie birds but have extended their range into man's artificial prairie. Others, the majority, are birds indigenous to the area where they originally occupied clearings in the

woods, wood margins and other zones resembling those of the modern farmland with hedges, scattered shrubs and gardens which have replaced them. These birds greatly increase in numbers if they are able to tolerate the proximity of—and disturbance by—man. Others, notably the larger birds of prey which have been persecuted and are less tolerant of man, have decreased.

The more common species found near farms are Eastern Kingbirds, Phoebes, which often nest on house ledges, Barn Swallows, Purple Martins, House Wrens and Catbirds. The proverbial Bluebird is often found literally in the backyard, although it has suffered from poisoning by insecticides as well as competition for nesting sites from Starlings and sparrows. The Common Grackle, which nests in colonies in pine trees, is very common and the nests of Eastern Meadowlarks can be found in the open field. The Red-winged Blackbird, or Redwing as it is commonly called, which is probably the most numerous North American bird, nests in marshes and reedbeds, but usually seeks its food in fields where it mixes with Starlings, Common Grackles and Brown-headed Cowbirds. The cowbird does not build a nest of its own, but lays its eggs in the nests of other birds such as Song Sparrow and Yellow Warbler. Although the young cowbird does not actively dislodge its step-siblings, its faster rate of growth makes it almost impossible for its step-parents to rear their own young successfully at the same time.

Hedgerows and wood margins harbor such brightly colored seed-eaters as Cardinals, Blue Grosbeaks and Indigo Buntings. The bright yellow American Goldfinch flocks around thistles and sun-

Left The Broad-winged Hawk, a forest inhabitant, abandons its solitary habits on migration and is often seen in flocks

Right Killdeers have benefited from the clearing of woodland. They are common on open fields near water

flowers. Sparrows, in a confusion of different, but similar-looking kinds find the open landscape ideal. Grasshopper, Vesper, Field, Chipping and Song Sparrows have all found their various niches to exploit and their songs are as much part of the spring and summer in the farmland as are those of the warblers in the woods.

Of the larger birds, Killdeers and occasionally Upland Plovers or Sandpipers may be encountered, but Bobwhites are more common and, in some areas, the introduced ornamental Ring-necked Pheasant. The omnipresent Common Crows abound as they will eat almost any kind of scrap which they can find.

Red-shouldered and Red-tailed Hawks may be seen soaring high above on the lookout for rodents, and the Sparrow Hawk, interrupting its flight to hover and check out a suspicious movement below, is common. Marsh Hawks may also be sighted as they course low over the fields. At night Barn Owls and Screech Owls prey upon the multitude of rodents feeding off the grain left by man.

The north-eastern section of this region contains many marshes and ponds in which cat-tails, bulrushes and sedges are common. These localities often harbor a large concentration of birds. Even the smallest marsh will have at least one nesting Redwing and in the larger ones the American Bittern, a member of the heron family, will reveal its presence by its deep hollow croaking. It might also be possible to catch a glimpse of its relative, the Least Bittern, as it climbs through the reeds. The majestic Great Blue Heron can be seen standing motionless at the water's edge waiting for a fish to come within striking distance. The small Green Heron prefers smaller ponds and streams, but is common throughout the area. Common Gallinules and Coots are rarely found far from the vegetation of the edge, although both are good swimmers. The Virginia Rail and its relative, the Sora, keep well-hidden among the sedges where both the Short-billed and Long-billed Marsh Wrens also have their homes. Pied-billed Grebes are quite common although not often seen. At the slightest sign of danger they will submerge and may stay under water with only the head above the surface. Where there are large bodies of open water, Black Terns can be seen in elegant flight chasing insects at the surface.

Wood Ducks seek their food in wooded ponds and wet marshes, and Tree Swallows and Rough-winged Swallows can be encouraged to breed with well-placed nest boxes. Depending on the amount of open water present, other ducks might also be attracted. The most common are the Mallard and the Black Ducks.

The southern swamps are among the most extensive and fascinating in North America. Stretching from the Atlantic coast across northern Florida towards the west, they are situated in, or just south of, the southern pine belt. These swamps, some of them with enormous stands of majestic cypresses, others with large marshes of pickerel weeds and ladderworts, also contain ponds and rivers of more open water.

In many areas drainage has destroyed much of this wilderness and lumbering has decimated the cypress forests. Only a fraction remains today in an area in which it would once have been possible to see flocks of Carolina Parakeets flying noisily above the treetops and Ivory-billed Woodpeckers exploring the tree trunks for insects. The Carolina Parakeet, the only parrot of North America, became extinct at the

Right Like its relatives, the cormorants, the Anhinga is often seen drying its wings in the sun

Below The brown stripes of the American Bittern camouflage it well in the reedbeds it frequents

beginning of this century and the Ivory-billed Woodpecker is, if still surviving, only found in isolated, inaccessible spots, and doomed to extinction. Both species depended heavily on the large tracts of undisturbed cypress forest, a landscape which no longer exists.

Although many songbirds are found in the cypress swamps, the open marshes offer the opportunity for seeing larger and more spectacular species of birds. Sandhill Cranes are common although far outnumbered by a variety of herons. Snowy Egrets, American Egrets and the recent invader, the Cattle Egret, flash their snow-white wings over the marsh as they move from one favored fishing spot to the

next. Little Blue Herons and Great Blue Herons are also numerous, as are the White Ibises with their long, red, curved bills.

The Anhinga, or Snake Bird, is a common bird here. The name 'Snake Bird' is derived from its habit of sometimes swimming with its body submerged and only its head and long snake-like neck above the surface. Chasing fish under water this long neck allows it to spear its unfortunate prey with a sudden darting movement of its sharp pointed bill. As the Anhinga emerges from the water and clambers to a branch to spread its wings to dry in the sun, one is reminded of a long-gone prehistoric era when reptiles dominated the earth. The alligators and the multitude of snakes and turtles found in the same habitat only reinforce this impression.

Another unique bird of the swamps is the Wood Ibis or Wood Stork. This is the only North American representative of this family of long-legged birds, a family much more common and widespread in the Old World. The Wood Ibises nest in colonies in tall cypress trees but are now only local in distribution and very susceptible to droughts. However, sanctuaries have been created for the preservation of this species, efforts which will, hopefully, be successful.

Although Ospreys and even Bald Eagles, as well as many species of hawks, may be found here, this is the area where the most graceful of all birds of prey can best be seen. This is the Swallow-tailed Kite. Its elegance as it slowly courses low over the tree tops on its lookout for lizards, frogs or other suitable prey, is unsurpassable. The long slender wings and the deeply forked tail combine with its white and black

plumage in the most exquisite way. Fortunately, this bird is not particularly rare compared with its relative, the Mississippi Kite, a much smaller and less spectacular bird of prey. The Mississippi Kite hunts insects in the air with a dexterity rarely surpassed by any other bird of prey.

Another feathered predator which is a common inhabitant of the southern swamps is the Barred Owl. Although found over most of eastern North America, this is the area where it reaches its greatest abundance. Unlike most other owls, this large and attractive-looking bird can often be seen perched on branches during the daylight hours. Its hooting is a characteristic sound of the night in the cypress swamps.

During the fall and spring the eastern forest is traversed by a large number of birds as they pass to and from their more northern breeding grounds. One of the great experiences of the birdwatcher is to observe the migration of birds of prey along the mountain slopes of the Appalachians. Here, particularly at Hawk Mountain in Pennsylvania, one can see pass by hundreds of birds of prey of a dozen different species as they use the strong updrafts to facilitate their travel towards the south.

Many northern species of birds find the eastern forest mild enough to allow them to winter in the area. Feeding stations as well as grainfields often help them survive this inhospitable season.

Wood Storks, the only North American storks, nest in tall cypress trees in the southeast

The East Coast

The east coast takes many different forms.

The rocky coast of the arctic continues south through the spruce belt and even into the area of the great eastern deciduous forest. Stretching from Labrador to Massachusetts the shores are cut by innumerable bays and fjords. Islands ranging in size from the 42,734 square miles of Newfoundland to the thousands of islets of only a few square feet lie immediately offshore. As these islands offer better protection from both man and other predators, they are favored as breeding grounds by an impressive number of seabirds.

The adjacent sea modifies the coastal climate. The sea currents running parallel to the coast equalize to a large degree the temperature changes from north to south. Life conditions are therefore only gradually changed as we move from north to south in this area.

Such northern species as murres or guillemots, Razorbills and Kittiwakes nest on Newfoundland and its surrounding islands. The breeding grounds of Black Guillemots, Puffins and Eider Ducks stretch even further south into Maine. Gannets inhabit some of the islands offshore, where the nesting grounds of Leach's Petrel are also found. This starling-sized seabird nests in holes in the turf and colonies may contain hundreds of nests, but are largely unobserved as the petrels only come to land during the night. At this time the females and males switch places and the incubating bird is relieved of its duty for a period of twenty-four to ninety-six hours during which time it finds its food far out to sea. When the young have hatched they too are only visited at night when they receive their ration of regurgitated food.

Off Newfoundland is Funk Island, famous for its once enormous colony of Great Auks. This flightless 'penguin' of the north was slaughtered in thousands by early fishermen who visited the rich Newfoundland fishing banks. Later the Great Auks were also killed for their feathers and it appears that the North American colony had already ceased to exist by 1800. The last Great Auk in the world to be killed met its end in Iceland in 1848.

The Newfoundland banks with their enormously rich marine life also support visitors from the Southern Hemisphere. In summer Great Shearwaters, Sooty Shearwaters and Wilson's Petrels, which all nest in the faraway South Atlantic, congregate here for their 'winter' and share the richness of the sea with the local breeding birds.

In winter the banks are visited by hundreds of thousands of murres, Kittiwakes, Razorbills, Little Auks, Fulmars and Puffins from arctic North America, including Greenland, and Iceland and northern

Migration of the Great Shearwater

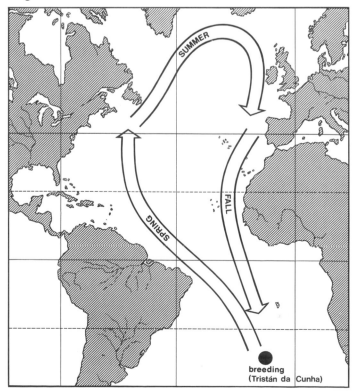

breeding
(Tristán da Cunha)

Right Like most mothers the female Razorbill guards its inquisitive young against the dangers of the environment

Below The nests of the Kittiwakes are precariously placed on tiny ledges on vertical cliffs

Europe. Even Kittiwakes from arctic Russia will travel to these banks. The Great Skua, a relative of the jaegers, comes here from Iceland and the British Isles and in recent years Black-headed Gulls from Iceland have become regular visitors to harbors and coasts of this region.

South of Maine most of the Atlantic coast consists of sandy beaches, often with large dunes, protecting a belt of marshes and bays against the ever-rolling swells of the Atlantic. This wall of sand is continually changing as wind and currents move hundreds of tons of sand every day. Yet the marshes behind it are relatively well protected and the low still water supports a rich variety of life. At different points along the coast the marshes vary from a few yards to miles in width before they meet the higher and dryer land of the solid continent itself.

The most characteristic birds of the whole coastal area are the many gulls which, in seemingly countless numbers, patrol beaches, marshes and harbors. Herring Gulls are very common and the larger and more vociferous Greater Black-backed Gulls are slowly extending their range southwards. The nesting colonies of these gulls are found on islands and more protected beaches. They often number hundreds of birds and the air above such a colony is a continuous roar of gulls crying and mewing. The gray-spotted young are constantly begging for food, their appetite apparently without bounds. Cannibalism is not uncommon, but it is usually the youngest and weakest chicks which end their lives as food for their own kind. A large percentage of the food consumed by these gulls consists of shellfish such as clams and mussels. To break the shell the gull will carry it aloft in its beak and drop it on a stone or hard-surfaced road to shatter. The garbage dumps of coastal cities and the surplus from the fishing fleets have combined to give the opportunity for an almost incomparable spread of these gulls.

In the marshes behind the sand barrier, as well as on islands, there are large breeding colonies of Laughing Gulls. This black-headed, medium-sized gull is less of a scavenger than the Herring Gull. Its food consists mainly of worms, insects and crabs found in marshes and along the beach.

On the sandy beach itself Fish Crows, close kin of the Common Crow, compete with the gulls for the flotsam generously washed ashore by the sea.

There are only a few species which nest actually in the sand of the open beach. One is the elegant Least or Little Tern. Unfortunately this lively little bird with its angry call has suffered much from man's interest in its habitat. The Least Tern has had to abandon many of its breeding sites for the summer crowd of bathers who enjoy the coolness of the seashore. Piping Plover and Semi-palmated Plover can also be found nesting on the beaches as can the larger Wilson's Plover further south, but they, as most other shorebirds, prefer the better protected upper beaches, where there are also colonies of other terns. The Common Tern is the most numerous. Colonies may consist of several hundred nests, but more often they are smaller. Sometimes Arctic Terns and Roseate Terns nest within the colonies.

The terns' habit of nesting in groups is of definite advantage to the species. Herring Gulls, Crows, dogs and other predators are chased away from the area by a spirited mass attack which from a single pair would have little chance of protecting the nesting site efficiently. Other birds sometimes take advantage of this relative security and it is not uncommon to find duck nests among the brooding terns. The spread of the Herring Gull has, however, become a real threat to these graceful birds, although much less so than the mass slaughter of fifty to a hundred years ago when the white feathers of the terns were sought for the millinery industry. A new threat is poisoning by insecticides washed off the land into both fresh water and the sea. Here fish accumulate the poison and through them it reaches the fish-eating birds. Although the concentration of poison is not enough to kill a bird outright, there is mounting evidence that sub-lethal doses can cause birth defects in the young. Abnormalities such as multiple feet, absent tail feathers and stunted wings have been described in the Common Tern.

Further south other species of terns become common. For example, the Sandwich Tern, which is considerably larger than the Common Tern, often nests in very dense colonies with the even larger Royal Tern. Forster's Tern, although it looks quite similar to the Common Tern, has less affinity to the seashore and may often be seen hawking insects over marshes and fields.

The largest of the terns is the Caspian; it is almost the size of a Herring Gull and has a wingspan of over four feet. Like the Herring Gull it does not refrain from supplementing its diet of fish with eggs and smaller birds. It is confined to the beaches to a lesser degree than most of the other terns and may be encountered far inland along rivers and lakes.

The main method by which terns obtain their food is by plunging headlong into the water and grabbing a fish which has ventured too close to the surface for its own good. As the terns patrol their hunting grounds they may make a sudden plunge or may be seen stopping to hover for a few seconds before making an attack on the unsuspecting prey below.

Akin to the terns is the strange Black Skimmer. It is a large, long-winged bird, black above and white below with a black-tipped red bill. It belongs to a small family of birds with unique bills as the lower mandible is considerably longer than the upper. As the skimmer courses low above the surface of the water, it holds the tip of the lower mandible down in the water. This attracts small fish which are then caught as the bird retraces its course. Black Skimmers prefer the quiet bays behind the sand barrier for their hunting grounds. Much of their fishing takes place late in the day as the light is waning and the fish move closer to the surface.

In the extensive marshes along the shore the Willet is the most common breeding shorebird, while in the bays the American Oystercatcher may be encountered. It is sometimes possible to catch a glimpse of the Clapper Rail in the ditches and inlets as it searches the mud for crabs and insects. The Clapper Rail is very similar to the King Rail, but whereas the Clapper Rail is an almost exclusively salt marsh bird, the King Rail strongly prefers the freshwater marshes.

Seaside Sparrows and Sharp-tailed Sparrows are among the few passerines found in this habitat so strongly dominated by waterbirds.

The east coast is known for its many Ospreys. This is a magnificent bird of prey which lives solely on the fish it catches by diving feet first into the water, grasping the prey with its sharp talons. In some areas—the Delaware Bay region, for instance—veritable colonies of nesting Ospreys are found, but

Soon the young Sandwich Tern begging food from its parents will have to do its own fishing as it is almost ready to fend for itself

in most places it is a solitary nester. The nest is placed preferably in a pine tree in the open, but telegraph poles or other artificial sites are sometimes used. An old wagon wheel placed on the top of a stake might well entice a pair of Ospreys to nest— they have even been found nesting on top of a working crane.

As for so many birds, the widespread use of insecticides now constitutes a real threat to this species; in recent decades it has disappeared from many localities and declined in others where it used to abound. Like the terns, the adult bird is not killed, but the poison causes changes in the formation of

the egg, making the shell much thinner than normally and therefore much more vulnerable to any sort of injury. This same effect on the eggs has been observed in Bald Eagles and Brown Pelicans, two other species largely dependent on fish for food.

Scattered along the entire east coast from Florida in the south to Long Island in the north are colonies of large wading birds, the herons and ibises. These colonies are usually found in groups of bushes or low trees in, or very close by, the marshes which supply the fish on which these birds live. The largest variety of species is found in the south where Brown Pelicans and Double-crested Cormorants may mix

The fish-eating Osprey is a characteristic inhabitant of the eastern seaboard where its bulky nest can be seen in many places

Right Gannets inhabit both sides of the Atlantic. This is part of the colony on Bonaventure Island

Below The most colorful gem of the southern swamps is the Purple Gallinule

Left Black Skimmers, relatives of the Terns, await the waning of daylight when the fish move close to the surface and are easier to catch

Below There is a mad scramble when more than one Brown Pelican spots a fish

with Snowy Egrets, American Egrets, Reddish Egrets, Cattle Egrets, Little Blue Herons, Yellow-crowned Night Herons and Glossy and White Ibises. Further north, the variety of species slowly declines and American, Snowy and Cattle Egrets together with Glossy Ibises and Black-crowned Night Herons come to dominate the heronries.

These heronries have gradually become much more common than they were at the beginning of this century. Hunting had decimated many species of herons to a degree where they were threatened with extinction, but a concerted effort by conservationists saved these stately birds. From the few colonies which remained they have been able to spread to their former haunts and regained lost ground. This spread is still occurring and many species are continuing to increase in numbers.

The Cattle Egret is a newcomer to North America, a newcomer as successful as the House Sparrow and Common Starlings introduced by man. Compared with these two species, the Cattle Egret appears to have crossed the Atlantic of its own accord. It reached South America from Africa in the 1930s and found its way from there to North America in the early 1950s. Since then it has spread with explosive speed and within twenty years it has been able to invade virtually the entire continent. It has obviously been able to fill an ecological niche previously not used by any native species. The Cattle Egret is much less bound to water than the other herons and a large part of its food consists of insects and even rodents and lizards caught in open dry land. The Cattle Egret derives its name from its habit of following grazing cattle, catching the insects flushed by the moving animal. In its African homeland it may often be seen perched on such large mammals as elephants and rhinoceroses as well as following these animals closely. It has brought this habit of following large mammals with it to North America. Although, undoubtedly, the agriculture of man has helped its spread, it is interesting to speculate what would have happened if the Cattle Egrets had crossed at an earlier time when herds of thousands of buffalo inhabited the prairies. At that time the Cattle Egret might have found the Bison indigenous to this continent as close an associate as today it finds our domesticated cattle.

The Gulf coast in most areas resembles the Atlantic, with an outer barrier of sandy islands or peninsulas protecting marshes and bays lying behind them. These wetlands reach even greater magnitude than along the Atlantic coast and the bird life is in some respects even richer. Although many species are the same, some—the Brown Pelican for example—are much more numerous here. Like the terns, the Brown Pelican is a fish-eating bird, catching its prey by diving headlong into the water. It will, however, also try to obtain food in other ways and in southern harbors competes with gulls for the scraps of fish thrown overboard by fishermen.

Double-crested Cormorants are common and the smaller Olivaceous Cormorant is found nesting on the western part of the coast. The same species of herons as on the east coast are common, but the Glossy Ibis is replaced by the very similar White-faced Ibis.

It is also along the Gulf coast that it is possible to see the magnificent, but still quite rare, Roseate Spoonbill. In beauty of color it is surpassed only by the Flamingo which, however, is but a rare visitor from colonies on the Caribbean Islands.

The Mottled Duck, very similar in habit and appearance to the Black Duck, is found nesting in these marshes, while the Fulvous Tree Duck is unique to the coastal marshes of the Gulf coast. It is a peculiarly long-legged, long-necked duck which finds most of its food in rice fields. It is almost exclusively nocturnal in its habits which is why it is often overlooked, even in areas where it may be quite numerous.

The Purple Gallinule is also found in these southern marshes. This species, which is closely related to the Common Gallinule, is the real gem of the marshland. Its metallically glistening plumage contrasting with its bright yellow legs in the setting of water-lilies and other floating plants through which it walks, makes it an unforgettable sight.

Another shorebird characteristic of the Gulf coast is the Black-necked Stilt. This black and white shorebird has extremely long red legs. It nests in loose colonies in or by marshes with patches of open water. It is an active feeder, but its disproportionally long legs give its grace a slightly comical slant. Nevertheless, it is one of the most attractive of our shorebirds.

Important as the Atlantic and Gulf coasts may be as breeding grounds for the many species described above, the highest concentration of birds is found outside the breeding season. The marshes and bays are important wintering grounds for innumerable waterfowl. Almost every kind of surface-feeding duck, Pintails, Teals, Mallards, Baldpates, for example, can be met with here, and in the protected

The Black-necked Stilt, with its slightly comical grace, is a characteristic shorebird of the Gulf coast, although its distribution also extends southwards into Central and South America

bays Canvasbacks, Redheads, Scaups, Ring-necked Ducks, Buffleheads and Mergansers abound. Canada Geese, Brant Geese, Snow Geese and Whistling Swans feed in the larger bays and off the northern shores, where scoters and eiders are common.

During migration the marshes and beaches virtually swarm with a multitude of shorebirds on their way to or from their northern breeding grounds. Many of these shorebirds spend the winter along the coasts here, whereas others continue their travels to their wintering grounds in South America.

From a few stragglers arriving in South America in the 1930s the Cattle Egret has now spread over most of the New World

The Prairies

Through the center of North America, from the Gulf of Mexico well into southern Canada, stretches the wide belt of grasslands known as the prairies. When De Soto, as the first white man, ventured into this sea of grass in his vain search for gold and imaginary Indian cities of wealth to plunder, he commented on the vastness and inhospitality of the land. Yet he covered and saw only a fraction of this unique area.

In the east the prairies blend almost imperceptibly into the park-like western part of the large deciduous forest. In the west they are bordered by the huge Rocky Mountains which are both climatologically and biologically complex. The narrower northern border is the spruce belt. Here the dense forest slowly opens up and through a narrow belt of deciduous parkland gives way to the rolling hills of the prairies.

The prairie region, covering about 1,000,000 square miles, is not—and never was—as uniform as many imagine. Some parts are much dryer than others with consequent scant vegetation, while in other areas the grasslands are cluttered with lakes and cut by rivers. In some regions trees of various sorts have been able to get a foothold, breaking the monotony and offering possibilities for birds other than those restricted to the open grassland.

The prairies were, in part at least, maintained by a delicate natural balance in which three mammals played a major role: the herds of millions of Bison grazing there kept many of the plants besides the ubiquitous grass under control; the slightly comical Prairie Dogs which once inhabited this area in countless numbers kept the under surface relatively porous through their endless digging, and thus prevented the occasional torrential rain from lingering on the surface where it would have benefited trees and bushes; and the Pocket Gopher which lived on the roots of trees hindered their spread. The combined activities of these animals efficiently barred the forests of the east from claiming successfully a land in which many kinds of trees could otherwise have flourished.

During the last two centuries this natural balance has been radically altered. The Bison, ridiculously easy to kill with a gun, was barely saved from extinction at the beginning of this century. Its relatively small numbers are now confined to a few reservations. The Prairie Dogs, the 'towns' of which once covered thousands of square miles, are dwindling in numbers and the Pocket Gopher is also decreasing; its damage to trees is not confined to the ones unwanted by man. Farmers have limited these two animals very efficiently.

Vast areas of the prairies have been converted to farmland and only small parts remain in their natural state. Where the soil is suitable, cereals are grown and the less rich areas are fenced in and used for cattle. Many marshes and lakes have been drained for agricultural use.

This change into farmland in many ways resembles the change which took place in the western part of the deciduous forest belt and it is now often hard to say, even when traveling for hundreds of miles across the limit, where one ends and the other begins. In both areas farmsteads with planted trees and gardens—and often rather abundant fruit supply—offer ecological zones previously unknown in their present extent.

Where the two types of land meet, there is also a broad belt where eastern and western species of animals intermix, but these gradually replace each other as we move east towards the Atlantic or west towards the Pacific. Such a pair of species are the two meadowlarks, the Eastern Meadowlark with its breeding range reaching well west of the Great Lakes, and the Western Meadowlark which nests far into the Great Lakes region. The two birds are almost indistinguishable in look and habit and often winter in mixed flocks. Their songs, however, easily distinguish them. The Eastern has been described as a slurred whistle, the Western is characterized by a loud flute-like song. When transferred to paper as a sonagram the differences become even more obvious. Another pair of such species are the Western and the Eastern Kingbirds. The yellowish-brown Western Kingbird has a strong preference for open country with only a few stands of trees. The deforestation of the eastern deciduous forest belt has given it an opportunity to spread its range towards the east. For the Eastern Kingbird, on the other hand, which is more dependent on taller trees, the homesteads and farms with gardens on the formerly open prairie have offered it possibilities for spread westwards.

Some of the true prairie birds have been severely threatened by the cultivation of their once undisturbed grassland. Such is the case of the Greater Prairie Chicken. Although initially benefiting from the extensive agriculture of the first farms, the in-

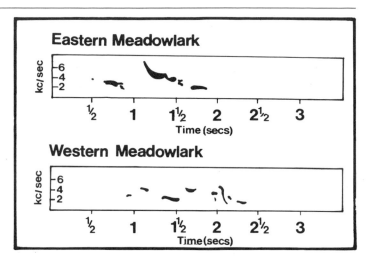

Eastern and Western Meadowlarks are practically indistinguishable in look and behavior and often winter in mixed flocks, but can be told apart by their songs as the sonograms show. Although their range sometimes overlaps there is no interbreeding; it is thought that song is the main isolating mechanism.

Below The display of the Sharp-tailed Grouse lacks nothing in vigor and splendor

Right The Sparrow Hawk is common in open country. It feeds on insects and rodents

tensification of land use has caused a decline which it is doubtful the species will survive. Its spectacular display may be one of the great scenes of nature future Americans will be unable to enjoy. In spring, males, sometimes as many as fifty together, congregate at dusk and at dawn. Here, on the traditional booming grounds, they display their splendor to win acceptance by one of the females in the area. As soon as mating has occurred the display continues and no true pair is formed. Often only a few of the males are accepted by the females, and most of the chickens hatched in one area have the same father although different mothers. Even closer to extinction is the Lesser Prairie Chicken. It is in many respects similar to the Greater Prairie Chicken, but adapted to the more southern and drier prairie landscapes. Only the strictest conservation measures will make it possible for this species to survive. The Sharp-tailed Grouse is more common. Although less spectacular, it too has display grounds where males assemble. In the sagebrush area on the western fringe of the prairies, the Sage Grouse may be found. This large colorful grouse, however, has its main distribution in the areas west of this region.

The ecological niche for gamebirds established by extensive agriculture has turned out to be a niche no native species has been able to fill. Instead, two introduced birds, the Ring-necked Pheasant and the Gray Partridge, now abound in the land reclaimed from the Bison and the Prairie Dogs. As in many other parts of the country, the Bobwhite has undoubtedly benefited from the farming, which provides more cover in an otherwise treeless plain. But even this hardy bird has difficulties in comparison to the two introduced species which, prior to their release in America, had hundreds of years in which to adjust to man and his ways in the Old World.

Characteristic of the original prairie was the Prairie Falcon. This stately bird has still been able to hold its own although in ever dwindling numbers. It is slightly smaller than the Peregrine Falcon and lighter in color. For nesting it prefers cliffs, where it finds inaccessible ledges on which to lay its five eggs. Its food consists of an assortment of small- to medium-sized birds but, where still present, Prairie Dog is its staple diet.

The smaller rodents are hunted by the almost ubiquitous Sparrow Hawk, the Red-tailed Hawk and the Ferruginous Hawk. The latter is very characteristic of the open grassland where it is frequently seen perched on poles or soaring low over the ground on the lookout for ground squirrels and other small rodents. As is the case with several species of hawks of the *Buteo* group, it occurs in two distinct color

The Horned Lark is the only representative of a family widespread in the Old World

phases, a dark and a light. The biological advantage of this phenomenon is unknown. The same two color phases occur in Swainson's Hawk, the common hawk of the open country in the west. This hawk, slightly smaller than the Ferruginous Hawk, lives on insects to a larger degree. Although both birds are directly beneficial to man in his fight against crop-destroying rodents and insects, both species have been, and in some areas still are, hunted by the very farmers and ranchers they assist. Luckily they have been able to survive in reasonable numbers so they are not threatened by extinction. Another bird which preys on the many rodents is the Prairie Owl. This small, short-tailed but long-legged owl nests on the ground in abandoned Prairie Dog holes. It is often seen sitting in front of its hole during the daytime. when it is possible to observe its curious habit of slowly closing one eye at a time, as if it were winking at the observer. Like the Prairie Dog, it has undergone a drastic decline in numbers.

The Turkey Vulture is, as in most of North America, not uncommon. As in other areas, it is often seen near roads and highways where many animals are unnoticed victims of traffic. In their hunger for a killed animal on the road, the vultures themselves not infrequently fall prey to the dangers of fast-moving vehicles.

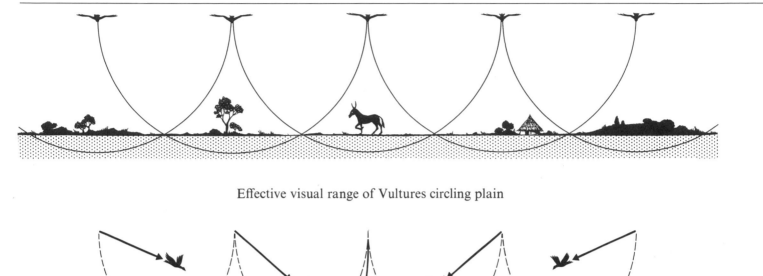

Effective visual range of Vultures circling plain

Carcass noted by center bird. Its descent is noted by immediately neighboring birds whose
descent is in turn noted by their neighbors

Vultures have sharp eyesight. As they soar high in the sky they are scattered over a considerable area and not only keep a keen eye open for possible carcasses on the ground, but also take note of their neighbors in the air. When a vulture notices a carcass on the ground, it drops down to examine it closer. This is noted by its neighbors who drop to see if there is enough for more than one. Their descent in turn is noted by others and soon, from an apparently empty sky, a whole flock of these black, sinister-looking birds has dropped.

The wild grassland supports its own roster of smaller birds—most living on the seed of the various grasses—such as Horned Larks, Chestnut-collared and McCown's Longspurs, Savannah, Sage, Baird's, Grasshopper, Clay-colored, Le Conte's, Sharp-tailed, Cassin's and Brewer's Sparrows, each with its own slightly different preference of surrounding. The Bobolink, a relative of the blackbirds and grackles, which migrates south in large flocks, nests commonly in the northern prairie.

Sprague's Pipit, the longspurs and the Horned Larks, represent families of birds which are much more widespread in the Old World, where grasslands are both geologically older and of much greater extent than in North America. Although not introduced, these birds are probably fairly recent

arrivals to the New World where the prairies offered them a suitable habitat.

Along the rivers where there are some trees and bushes and in the small wooded plots created by the agricultural activities of man, a number of birds not originally associated with the grasslands may be encountered. Many eastern species such as Eastern Pewee, Eastern Bluebird, Red-headed Woodpecker, Orchard and Baltimore Orioles, Cardinal, Catbird and Brown Thrasher are common. Others are species which are transcontinental in their distribution. Such species are Mourning Dove, Barn Swallow, Bank Swallow or Sand Martin and Rough-winged Swallow, Purple Martin, House Wren, Loggerhead Shrike, Chipping and Song Sparrows, Robin, Starling and Killdeer and, in the south, Blue Grosbeak and Summer Tanager. The more purely western species are the Western Wood Pewee, Say's Phoebe, Black-billed Magpie, Black-headed Grosbeak, Brewer's Blackbird and Rock Wren.

The Mountain Plover, a relative of the Golden Plover of the arctic, is common among low grass and on sandy plains.

Throughout the northern part of the prairie belt are innumerable marshes, ponds and lakes which in summer furnish a richness of waterbird, unsurpassed except by their more northern and undisturbed

A Western Grebe chick has found refuge on the back of
its parent while it attends its still unhatched siblings

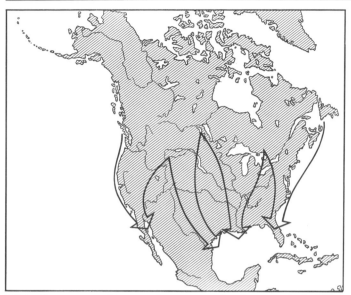

Main flyways used by northern waterfowl to reach their wintering grounds. From east to west they are called the Atlantic, the Mississippi, the Central and the Pacific flyways

counterparts. Here Western Grebes perform their spectacular courtship dances and 'runs' on the lakes and the more secretive Eared Grebe nests in colonies. White Pelicans and Double-crested Cormorants are common where the lakes are deep and large enough to have an ample supply of fish.

Ducks are very numerous. In this area are some of the main breeding grounds for Blue-winged and Green-winged Teals, Mallards, Pintails, Gadwalls and American Widgeon or Baldpates. The Shoveler with its wide flat bill skims the surface for insect larvae, snails and small floating plants, and Diving Ducks are also common. Redheads, Lesser Scaups and the funny-looking Ruddy Ducks search the shallow bottom for plants and occasional insects and other invertebrates, while Canvasbacks sift the mud for mollusks and roots. This latter species, because of its feeding habits, has become particularly prone

The prairie is the true homeland of the Sandhill Crane

Below The Canvasback, a favored gamebird, is a common
inhabitant of the prairie lakes

Bottom The splendor of the drake Mallard in its nuptial
plumage can hardly be surpassed

Below The Prairie Falcon nests on inaccessible cliffs in the west

Turkey Vultures live mainly on carcasses. In between their searching flights they rest in treetops

to lead poisoning as it swallows many of the pellets left from hunting. Fortunately, the limitations on commercial mass slaughter have restored many of these species to something vaguely resembling their former abundance and none is seriously threatened at the present time, although drainage has limited their breeding habitats.

Canada Geese are also common here and often occur in large flocks. The migration of these waterfowl has been thoroughly investigated and a simplified picture of the routes to and from the breeding grounds can be seen from the map on page sixty-one. This is based on the banding of birds carried out on a massive scale in the first half of this century; this is still being continued to learn more about the life histories of these attractive birds.

In the marshes there are shorebirds of various sorts, the most attractive of which is probably the American Avocet. This beautiful black and white wader obtains its food by skimming the surface of the water with sideway movements of its slightly upturned bill. Often a whole line of birds will walk side by side while feeding.

The most stately of the marsh birds is the Sandhill Crane. Once found nesting throughout the prairie, it is now more or less limited to the marshes where it places its nest on little hillocks, or builds platforms of dead vegetation. In spring when these elegant birds arrive in flocks from their southern wintering grounds, they can often be seen performing their dance, a curious slow mixture of jumps and bows performed by several birds simultaneously. A smaller population of Sandhill Cranes also exists in the interior of Florida and a larger population in the arctic, but the vanishing prairie is the true homeland of this species.

Other shorebirds met with in the marshes are Willet, Spotted Sandpiper, Wilson's Phalarope, Long-billed Curlew and Marbled Godwit.

This interior even harbors members of the otherwise mainly coastal family of gulls. The black-headed Franklin's Gull, Ring-billed Gull and California Gull nest here, and even the Common Tern breeds in colonies in suitable places. The California Gull is famed for its rescue of the Mormon colony in Utah when flocks of gulls attacked the grasshoppers plaguing the settlers.

Although drastically changed and with only poor remnants of its former glory, the prairie land still has its attractions for birdwatchers. If intelligent wildlife management, paired with strict conservation policies, prevails in the future, at least samples of this great and once far-reaching habitat should be preserved for future generations to enjoy.

The fragile elegance of the American Avocet leaves an indelible impression once it has been observed

The Temperate Rain Forest

From Kodiak Island in Alaska almost all the way to the Gulf of San Francisco there is a long, relatively narrow belt of unique forest along the coast. This forest, dominated by Douglas Fir, is mainly coniferous but also includes a multitude of deciduous trees as well; many trees, such as the Redwoods, are of giant size and there is a luxuriant underbrush.

This forest, called the temperate rain forest, hugs the mountains which rise steeply from the coast. It is actually this combination of high mountains close to the coast and a current of warm water in the sea over which moist air forms which gives rise to this luxuriant vegetation. As the moist air is forced upward by the mountains, it is condensed and falls as heavy rain. This rainfall in some areas reaches more than 100 inches.

In the high mountains, however, the climate becomes colder and alpine flora and fauna, quite akin to that of the arctic, replace the luxuriant forest below. By the time the air has crossed these mountains it has given up most of its moisture and the rainfall on the eastern slopes of the mountains is therefore relatively scant. At the southern end of this belt, for instance, the east side of the mountains is bordered by a dry landscape of sagebrush; further north, the eastern slopes of the mountains blend into the spruce belt.

The temperate rain forest, in all its magnificence, has not escaped the effects of the most destructive of all animals, man. Lumbering is widespread, particularly in the south, and in many of the valleys the woods have been cleared to make way for agricultural land. Most of the northern part is still undisturbed, but there is a severe danger of the southern half of the forest being completely destroyed by man's short-sighted policy of profit making.

Although the birdlife of this lush forest in many respects resembles that of the spruce forest east of

California Quails make their homes in clearings in the rain forest

the mountains, it harbors many species especially adapted for and mainly found in this habitat.

In the lakes and rivers there are Wood Ducks, Harlequin Ducks, Barrow's Goldeneyes and Common Mergansers, all of which are also found east of the mountains. The birds of prey, such as Goshawk and Sharp-shinned Hawk, are mainly the same as those found in the spruce belt.

Of gamebirds, the Ruffed Grouse is common and in the south the California Quail abounds where it can find clearings in the woods, or where these have been provided by the establishment of small farmsteads. The Great Blue Heron nests in colonies in trees by lakes.

The Band-tailed Pigeon is common. Although its stock was once decimated by hunting, protection has secured its return in numbers. It has often been accused of doing severe damage to the grain crop by local farmers, but scientific investigations have not been able to substantiate these claims. The Mourning Dove is also common here, as in most of North America, but particularly in more open landscapes and near homesteads and farms.

The Great Horned Owl and the Screech Owl, both widespread on the North American continent, are inhabitants of the forest also. Unique to the west coast, however, are the rather large Spotted Owl, the western counterpart of the Barred Owl, and the tiny Pygmy Owl. Compared with most other owls, Pygmy Owls are active during the day; they live largely on insects.

Four species of swifts are found exclusively in western North America, and two of these are found in the rain forest. The Black Swift is the largest of all the North American swifts. It places its nest in deep crevices in mountain canyons often near—or even behind—high waterfalls so that the nest is constantly exposed to extremely moist air. Vaux's Swift nests in hollow trees, preferred sites being the huge hollowed out Redwoods. Like all swifts, it is an excellent flier and is often seen flying high and extremely fast in its pursuit of insects. In recent years Vaux's Swift has started nesting in chimneys. As the forester leaves fewer and fewer hollow trees standing, the survival of this species may depend on its ability to adapt successfully to the use of these artificial sites.

One species of hummingbird, a family usually associated with the tropics, breeds throughout the rain forest as far north as Alaska. This is the Rufous Hummingbird, a pugnacious little fellow able to chase enemies many times its size away from its nesting site.

The woods support several kinds of woodpeckers; the large Pileated and the much smaller Hairy,

Downy and Northern Three-toed Woodpeckers, all of which are also found in other parts of North America. The Red-shafted Flicker is the western counterpart of the Yellow-shafted Flicker and shares the species' preference for ants.

Of the flycatchers, Traill's and the Olive-sided Flycatchers extend their range from the spruce belt into the rain forest where they meet Hammond's and Western Flycatchers, which are both indigenous to this region as is the Western Wood Pewee. Both the Tree Swallow, common across the continent, and the western Violet-green Swallow nest in tree cavities. They are commonly seen dashing through the air catching insects.

Steller's Jay, in this region as in most of the west, replaces the Blue Jay so abundant in the east. In open areas the Black-billed Magpie, Common Crow, Raven and small Northwestern Crow can be found. This latter species never ventures far from the beach and is a western counterpart to the Fish Crow common along the eastern seashore.

One of the most numerous species of the rain forest is the Chestnut-backed Chickadee. Like other chickadees, it nests in tree cavities and outside the breeding season it moves about in small flocks searching the pine trees for insects. In more open

Although small these two young Rufous Hummingbirds find their quarters crammed

The Great Blue Heron is one of the largest, most widely distributed and best known American herons. It is gregarious and often nests in large mixed colonies comprising several species

Right The enormous bill of the Evening Grosbeak is superbly suited for cracking seeds open

Below The Western Tanager usually frequents the tree tops but its song attracts attention

Opposite The Wood Duck drake is the most colorful of North American ducks

areas, often in gardens and parks, the Common Bushtit is found. This charming little bird weaves a pendent nest with an opening at the top in which it lays its four to eight eggs. Outside the nesting time it is, as the chickadees, quite social in its behavior.

The small Brown or Tree Creeper is quite inconspicuous as it searches the tree trunks for insects. Climbing upwards in spirals, it is able to cover large parts of the trunk and, like the more conspicuous Red-breasted Nuthatch, is as common here as in other coniferous forests. Small birds seem to thrive in this luxuriant habitat. The Winter Wren, only slightly more than three inches long, scurries about in the underbush. Its beautiful song fills the canyons and is of a volume far out of proportion to the small size of the bird. In the treetops Golden-crowned and Ruby-crowned Kinglets, which are only slightly larger than the Winter Wren, find their homes and build their domed nests. They share their insect-eating habits with warblers such as the Orange-crowned, Audubon's and Townsend's Warblers

The Brown Creeper builds its nest in crevices in the bark of large trees. This bird is bringing food to its young

which are all common in this region. But larger and more colorful songbirds can also be encountered. Thrushes are common, the Varied Thrush being indigenous to the region. Swainson's and Hermit Thrushes, as well as Robins, are also found here. In spring the Western Tanager, the male yellow with bright red head, fills the air with its Robin-like song.

Seed-eaters are very much the same as those found in the larger ecological zone of the spruce belt to the east: Pine Siskins, Crossbills, Evening Grosbeaks, Pine Grosbeaks and Fox Sparrows are abundant. Only the Oregon Junco and the Golden-crowned Sparrow, both common birds, are unique to the area. Cassin's Finch, more numerous further south and in more open country, can also be found in the rain forest.

Along the mountain streams here, as well as in the other western mountains, the Dipper can be seen. This thrush-sized relative of the wren is completely dependent on fast-running streams. It swims well but its food is obtained by running on the floor of the stream, where it finds aquatic insects and snails, holding on to the bottom with its strong toes. Its nest is most often found near waterfalls and is often placed behind the waterfall so that the Dipper has to fly through the falling water to get to and from the nest. This obviously offers good protection against many predators, most of which shun the effort needed to reach it.

Higher up the mountains the trees become smaller and the forest thins out, finally giving way to open tundra-like landscapes. Even higher the mountain peaks are covered in snow all the year round.

This open landscape has a birdlife of its own. In the north Willow and Rock Ptarmigans replace the White-tailed Ptarmigan which is found further south. Water Pipits have invaded the area from the arctic and the mountain tops are inhabited by Gray-crowned Rosy Finches which seek their food—insects and seeds—among the boulders and crevices. The valleys act as efficient barriers between separate populations of these birds and, like birds on islands, they have developed locally, giving rise to many different subspecies. The populations found in the high mountains further south, the Black Rosy Finch and the Brown-capped Rosy Finch, are even recognized as belonging to different species.

As in other high mountains in the west, the Mountain Bluebird is also found although not at such high altitudes as the more arctic species.

The uniqueness and magnificent beauty of the temperate rain forest, backed by snow-capped mountains, fully reward anyone who has the opportunity to visit it.

The Western Mountains

The northern part of the western mountains has been described in the preceding chapters: the western slope which forms the temperate rain forest, and the eastern which forms part of the transcontinental spruce belt.

As the enormous mountain chain of which the Rocky Mountains are part is followed southward, however, it swings away from the Pacific coast and crosses the United States in a long arc to close in on the Pacific coast in Mexico, south of the area with which we are here concerned. Meanwhile, along the Pacific coast of the United States there are ranges of other mountains, of which Sierra Nevada is the most impressive in height and length. Towards the east the Rockies meet the prairies, to the west the coastal ranges border on the Pacific Ocean. Between the two mountain chains, like an enormous bowl, is the Great Basin. This relatively high plateau is criss-crossed by many mountain chains, valleys and streams. Most of the area is drained by the Colorado River, breaking through the mountain rim through the spectacular Grand Canyon to the south and the Columbia River to the north.

This enormous area is extremely varied. Geographical factors in the form of the mountains themselves and the climatic change from the temperate zone in the north to the subtropical in the south combine with great variations in rainfall to form a maze of ecological zones quite different from the striking uniformity of, for instance, the spruce belt. The landscape is ever changing—from flat deserts to deep valleys and soaring mountains, from pine forests to cactus plains.

In this varied landscape there is an equal variation in birdlife. A mountain climb will bring one through zones which in flat country would take days and weeks to traverse and thus the birdwatcher is in the company of constantly changing species of birds.

The semi-diagramatic illustration on this page gives an idea of the changes in landscape, over simplified as it may be.

THE MONTANE CONIFEROUS REGION

Along the ridges of the mountains, particularly in the north, there are areas covered by snow and ice all year round. On the alpine tundra below these peaks live the Water Pipits, Rosy Finches and White-tailed Ptarmigans, while further down is the montane coniferous region. Roughly, this ecological zone forms an interrupted circle around the Great Basin

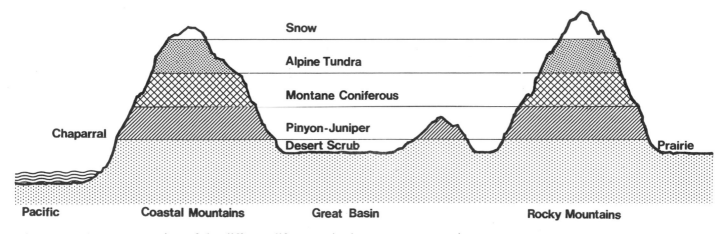

Diagrammatic representation of the different life zones in the western mountains

and its birdlife is to some degree influenced by where on the circle the birdwatcher is standing. For example, there are some differences between the northern and southern segments of the circle.

In the north the birds are mainly the same as those found in the spruce belt and the temperate rain forest. Blue, Spruce, and Ruffed Grouse are common, as is the Pygmy Owl. The Great Gray Owl, an inhabitant of the northwestern spruce belt, even reaches this far south and the transcontinental Saw-whet Owl is also met with here. The White-throated Swift may be seen along rugged cliffs and canyons. Besides the woodpeckers of the spruce belt, the relatively rare, but in the west widespread, Williamson's Sapsucker may be observed. Its habits resemble those of the Yellow-bellied Sapsucker, but the great difference in plumage between the sexes makes it unique among woodpeckers. Members of the flycatcher and swallow families are also the same as those found to the north. Steller's Jay and the Gray Jay are found in most of the montane coniferous forest, as is Clark's Nutcracker. This gray bird, with flashingly contrasting black and white wings and tail, was named after the famous companion of Lewis who explored this region in the early nineteenth century. It often visits campsites for scraps of food, but otherwise eats a varied diet of acorns, fruits and insects. Throughout the coniferous forest the Mountain Chickadee is common. It resembles the widespread Black-capped Chickadee, but has a distinct white stripe above the eye. No less than three species of nuthatch are also found here: White-breasted, Red-breasted and Pygmy. Brown Creepers and both species of kinglet are common. The thrushes are the same as those found in the temperate rain forest. Orange-crowned, Audubon's, Townsend's and MacGillivray's Warblers are common. The Western Tanager is found throughout the western coniferous belt as are the Evening Grosbeak, Cassin's Finch, Pine Grosbeak, Pine Siskin, Red Crossbill and Fox Sparrow. The Oregon Junco is in the south replaced by the Gray-headed and Mexican Juncos.

The southern coniferous forest differs somewhat in its birdlife in that, in addition to the species already mentioned, we might find such birds as Olive, Virginia, and Red-faced Warblers and the Painted Redstart.

It is in the zone of montane coniferous forest in the northeastern segment of the circle that there are many lakes and marshes harboring such species as White Pelicans, California Gulls and Caspian Terns, Western Grebes, Pintails, Teals and Hooded Mergansers. These lakes show an obvious and very close

The black, gray and white pattern of Clark's Nutcracker is beautifully fitting for the landscape it inhabits

affinity to those of the spruce belt as well as to the neighboring northern part of the prairies.

THE PINYON-JUNIPER ZONE

Deeper into the bowl of the basin, particularly in the southern half, there is an area of open park-like woodland where the main trees are pinyons and junipers. This type of landscape is not limited to the rim of the Great Basin, but also occurs in many of the mountains which are found between the Rocky Mountains and the coastal ranges.

Below this the landscape may pass directly into scrubland with sagebrushes or, further south, into deserts dominated by cacti. It may also, however, particularly along rivers and streams, blend into a more lush country with evergreen oaks and other shade trees. In some dryer southern areas it blends into a denser brushland of scrub-oak and sumac which forms a virtual chaparral. In this area there are a large number of different species of birds.

Parts of these landscapes lie on the southern border of the area treated in this book and many of the birds have their main distribution south of it. Examples of such species are the Black Hawk so common in Mexico, Zone-tailed Hawk, White-winged Dove, Lesser Nighthawk, Blue-throated and

Burrowing Owls often nest in Prairie Dog 'towns'. The nest is well protected by the pugnacious parents

Broad-billed Hummingbirds, Arizona Woodpecker, Olivaceous Flycatcher, the brilliantly colored Vermilion Flycatcher, Mexican Jay, Bridled Titmouse, Painted Redstart, Hepatic Tanager, Pyrrhuloxia and Rufous-crowned Sparrow.

Much more widespread in the pinyon-juniper zone and its neighboring stands of trees are such birds as Red-tailed, Swainson's and Sparrow Hawks. Two quails, the Mountain Quail and the Harlequin Quail are common. The Mountain Quail is the largest of North American quails and is a shy bird which, when disturbed, usually runs for cover under bushes and thickets. The Harlequin Quail, on the contrary, freezes on the spot where surprised, relying on its camouflage coloration for protection. In this area it is also possible to find remnants of the once widespread Turkey population. This species, preferred by Benjamin Franklin as a symbol of the United States, is now being reintroduced in many of its former haunts in the east from which it has disappeared. Many of these attempts have been quite successful and this interesting bird can now be seen in many areas of the southern part of North America.

Band-tailed Pigeons, as well as the ubiquitous Mourning Dove, are common. The Screech Owl and Great Horned Owl also find suitable habitats here, as does the Common Nighthawk. Closely related to the Nighthawk is the Poor-will, so named from its call. This latter species is unique as it is the only bird which has been proved to hibernate in the same fashion as many mammals. During cold spells it has been found in rock crevices in a torpid state and with a body temperature close to that of the surrounding air, and well below the normal body temperature of the Poor-will. This fact has probably been known for a long time by the local Hopi Indians in whose language the name for the species means 'the sleeper'. Other birds closely related to the Poor-will, such as swifts and hummingbirds, are known to be able to lower their metabolic rates for shorter periods of time. This may happen to swifts during long periods of bad weather which make it impossible for them to hunt insects. In hummingbirds it happens during the night.

Broad-tailed and Black-chinned Hummingbirds are common. The Broad-tailed Hummingbird also reaches higher elevations into the coniferous forest where it is often seen hovering in front of pine branches in search of insects. It is thus less dependent on flowering plants than most other hummingbirds. The Acorn or California Woodpecker is also often found in the high elevation. This striking black and white bird drills holes in trees to accommodate the acorns which it stores there. Lewis' Woodpecker has adopted the flycatching habits of the flycatchers. It is often seen perched high in a tree on the lookout

for flying insects. It also lives on other things, however, and, like the Acorn Woodpecker, often makes stores of acorns. Lewis' Woodpeckers, however, use natural crevices for this purpose.

Several species of the flycatcher family are represented. Western and Cassin's Kingbird are common as are Ash-throated and Gray Flycatchers.

In some areas Pinyon and Scrub Jays are abundant, both mainly blue and easily noticed.

Of smaller songbirds, Plain Titmouse, Bushtit, Bewick's Wren, Blue-gray Gnatcatcher, Gray Vireo, Black-throated Gray Warbler, Rufous-sided and Brown Towhee are among those commonly seen.

THE DESERT SCRUBLAND

As our descent continues, we now reach the bottom of the bowl of the Great Basin, the plateau itself. This consists of dry scrubland, often interrupted by lower mountain ranges, smaller rivers and, in some places, deserts. The northern and largest area is covered with sagebrushes which are usually from two to five feet in height. In this relatively dry landscape agriculture is very difficult, but cattle can be raised in some areas and sheep have also been introduced and have destroyed many parts. Most of the area, however, is relatively untouched by man.

The birdlife is not particularly rich, but certain species are specialized for this uninviting landscape. Such a species is the Sage Grouse. This is a large, long-tailed gamebird with a distinct black belly. To a large degree it lives on the surprisingly nutritious buds and leaves of the dry-looking sagebrushes. It is usually met in flocks, often composed of birds of the same age and sex. In spring the males, as in many other kinds of grouse, assemble on special display grounds where they try vigorously to attract the attention of visiting females by spectacular strutting, at the same time inflating the two yellow throat pouches and raising and fanning the tail, all the while uttering deep bubbling notes. During the hot summer months the Sage Grouse is found mainly along the mountain slopes, moving into the flat desert in winter. A European gamebird, the Chukar, has been successfully introduced and is now common in many areas.

The Sage Thrasher, somewhat similar to the Brown Thrasher found in the east but smaller and grayer, is also well adapted to this shrubby scrub, as is the elusive Sage Sparrow. More common and easily seen than the latter is Brewer's Sparrow. Compared with the Sage Sparrow, which skulks low and deep

Wild Turkeys are being restored to many areas in which they have previously been exterminated

among the foliage, Brewer's Sparrow moves about more openly and often in small flocks. In summer its sweet song, composed of series of rapid trills, is a characteristic sound of the sagebrush desert. The Gray Flycatcher perches on top of the small bushes as it scans the air for flying insects, its preferred food.

Less specialized birds may also be seen in this inhospitable land. Turkey Vultures hang overhead on the lookout for carcasses. Poor-wills spend the day in the shade. Western Kingbirds and Loggerhead Shrikes are on their exposed lookouts for insects. The charming Burrowing Owl is quite commonly seen. From nearby mountains Prairie Falcons and Golden Eagles make excursions over the desert. In these mountains the birdwatcher may also find the Rock Wren which hides its nest in holes or crevices, and in well-protected canyons, the Canyon Wren. Cliff Swallows, widespread but quite local in their distribution, may also be encountered here.

In the south the sagebrush, or northern desert scrubland as it is also called, gives way to the southern desert scrubland. In this hot, dry and relatively flat area cacti of various forms, together with other xerophytic plants, predominate.

The birdlife is quite rich in spite of the name desert ascribed to the region. Many species, most of them with a wider distribution south of the border, can well sustain the dryness and the heat and the mighty Saguaro cactus in many areas plays the role of the trees of the more northern lands. Sometimes these cacti are even large enough to support the bulky nest of the Red-tailed Hawk.

Two woodpeckers play an important role in the local ecology. These are the Gilded Flicker and the Gila Woodpecker. Both excavate their nesting holes in the Saguaro cacti. These holes are then used by a lot of other birds as well as other animals for shelter. This is particularly true of the Gila Woodpecker which makes holes in abundance far surpassing its own needs. Sparrow Hawks, the tiny insect-eating Elf Owl, Purple Martins, Ash-throated and Wied's Crested or Mexican Flycatchers all use old woodpecker holes for nesting sites.

The Cactus Wren, the largest North American wren, builds its football-sized domed nest in the branches of the cacti. Its song, which it gives persistently from an exposed spot even at the almost unbearable heat of noon, is rather unmusical, but a characteristic sound of the desert. The Crissal Thrasher, on the other hand, does not sing in the middle of the day. Both it and its relative, the Curved-billed Thrasher, seek their food on the ground and only sing in the cooler hours of dusk and dawn. On the ground one may also encounter one of the

The Gila Woodpecker plays an
important part in the ecology of the
desert scrubland; its superfluous
nesting holes are used by many
different birds, and also as a shelter
for other small animals

Top left Like many gallinaceous birds, the Sage Grouse has a very spectacular display

Bottom left Swainson's Hawk lives mainly on rodents, insects and reptiles found in the open country

Below The Barn Swallow is one of the species which has been able to adapt successfully to coexistence with man. It is widespread in the west and in many other parts of America

strangest of North American birds, the Road-runner. This gray-striped bird uses its long tail and short wings more for steering while running on the ground than for flying, which it rarely does. It is a relative of the cuckoos and shares their meat-eating habits, but instead of limiting itself to defenseless larvae, the Roadrunner eats a varied diet of scorpions, snakes, lizards and rodents. Its strong bill is a formidable weapon, unsuspected in a bird with such a comical appearance. It has the habit of slowly raising its crest and tail. The speed with which it can run—it easily outruns a man—has earned it its name.

Gambel's Quail is common. It closely resembles the California Quail. It is less well adapted to the dryness of the region than many other of the birds and therefore most often found near water, where this is present.

Of smaller birds found in this region, the Verdin, Costa's Hummingbird and the Desert Sparrow are species found almost exclusively in this habitat.

CHAPARRAL

In the southwest along the outer edge of the big bowl formed by the western mountains and roughly corresponding to southern California, there is yet another ecological region, the so-called chaparral. On the mountain slopes there are densely growing, relatively low trees and shrubs such as scrub oak, poison oak and buckthorns. By and large the climate is relatively dry. This area, particularly in the foothills, has been changed considerably by man's activity. Irrigation has made much of the area fertile and, more so than in the valleys, the change has been an improvement in the natural habitat. Many more flowering plants and bushes and water-loving shrubs have been able to thrive. This has certainly benefited many of the hummingbirds which have also taken advantage of the many flowers found in gardens and parks of the residential areas which have grown up. Such species as Broad-tailed, Anna's, Black-chinned, Allen's and, the tiniest of them all with a total length of only two and three quarter inches, Calliope Hummingbirds abound. The distinct court-ship display in which they fly back and forth like a pendulum is often seen and their chittering calls often draw attention to them. Their wing beats are very fast and they are the only birds which, in the fashion of helicopters, can fly backwards. All live on insects and nectar obtained from flowers in front of which they hover. Many are easily attracted to special feeders filled with sugar water.

The dry chaparral itself, however, has other birds which are characteristic. Flocks of the small, plain-colored Bushtits are commonly seen as they move from tree to tree in their search for insect food. The

dark brown Wrentit, on the contrary, is sedentary and keeps well hidden in the dense foliage. Bewick's Wren, with its habit of jerking its tail from side to side, is also common. The California Thrasher, with its long curved bill, finds its food on the ground. It uses its bill in finding insects hiding below the surface by literally pickaxing its way through the upper crust. This species shares the underbrush with the Brown Towee. Next to the hummingbirds, which are often called flying jewels, the Lazuli Bunting is the most colorful bird of this habitat. It has a wide distribution in the west where it replaces the Indigo Bunting of the east. The black and yellow Lesser Goldfinch is also common, usually encountered in small flocks.

Other species also found in other habitats may also be met with here, as for instance Orange-crowned Warbler, Rufous-crowned Sparrow, Sage Sparrow and Black-chinned Sparrow.

MAN IN THE WEST

When the Spaniards first arrived in the California valleys, they found them lush with marshes and grassland, the surrounding mountain slopes covered with chaparral. The change of the valleys into agricultural land started early. Irrigation of the dryer parts and the draining of marshes and lakes soon changed the landscape. Grainfields, orchards and vineyards sprang up, interspersed by residential areas. These latter have spread with explosive rapidity in this country, their gardens and parks offering new possibilities for the birds able to exploit them. In these areas today many of the same species are found which in other parts of the continent have been able to adjust themselves to the life-zones created by man. Widespread species are Sparrow Hawk, Mourning Dove, Barn Owl, Barn Swallow, Common Crow, Mockingbird, Robin, Yellow Warbler, Rufous-sided Towhee and Song Sparrows.

More local western species, such as the hummingbirds already mentioned, have also found their niches in this man-made landscape. The California Quail with its slightly ridiculous-looking, but charming, headplume is so abundant it has become the state bird of California. The Red-shafted Flicker and even Gilded Flickers may be found within the limits of many cities and towns. Western Kingbirds and Black Phoebes are common around farmsteads. The Black-billed Magpie, as well as the very local Yellow-billed Magpie, build their domed nests in trees near open fields. Bushtits, White-crowned Sparrows, Goldfinches and House Finches abound in shrubbery, and shade trees give cover for such colorful species as Bullocks and Hooded Orioles. On almost all California lawns Brown Towhees are common and in the open fields the Western Meadowlark competes with Brewer's Blackbird in abundance. Killdeers can also be found nesting in this habitat.

In the northern part of the Great Basin where agriculture has been possible many, although not all, of the species mentioned above are found. To this list, however, must be added such species as Mountain Bluebird, Black-headed Grosbeak, Say's Phoebe and, in the fields, Horned Larks.

In the valleys of California only small areas of the original wetlands still exist, now mainly as wildlife preserves. Besides the many species of herons also found elsewhere in North America, many of the species of ducks and shorebirds more abundant in the north can be found nesting here. These areas and the surrounding fields, however, are more important as wintering grounds for the many millions of waterfowl migrating here from their northern breeding grounds. Geese, ducks and swans abound in almost unimaginable numbers in these marshes and ponds.

One species indigenous to this area has suffered tremendously from man's short-sightedness, however. This is the California Condor, the world's largest flying bird, with a wingspan of up to nine feet. This bird was once widespread in the west, although probably never numerous. It now has a population of about fifty at which level it has remained stable for almost half a century. As one pair, at best, can rear only one chick every second year, its survival is extremely doubtful. Rigid protection has been able to keep the population at a stable level, but it takes little imagination to fear even minor changes in the environment which could make this magnificent bird join the sad list of animals never to be seen again on the surface of this earth.

The Roadrunner rarely flies. It relies on its strong legs for locomotion and its equally strong bill for obtaining the reptiles on which it mainly lives

The California Condor is the world's largest flying bird.
It is precariously close to extinction

The West Coast

From the arctic shores of Alaska the Pacific coast of North America stretches southward. The coast is dominated by the proximity of the great mountain chains which in many areas rise straight from the water's edge. Many small rocky islands lie just offshore offering protected breeding grounds for many species of seabirds. In some areas the rocky shore is interrupted by stretches of sandy beaches. Mudflats and salt marshes are relatively uncommon.

These features make the western shoreline distinctively different from the eastern coast of the North American continent. Although some of the breeding birds are the same as those encountered on the Atlantic side of the continent, more are different as the Pacific Ocean is well isolated from the Atlantic by the large landmasses of the Americas.

Petrels nest along the coast, almost exclusively on offshore islands. The most abundant is the Fork-tailed Petrel which ranges from the Aleutians to northern California. This almost white little bird nests, like other petrels, in holes in the turf which it visits at night only. Leach's Petrel, also found in the North Atlantic, is more widespread, its breeding range stretching along the entire coast. It is, however, much less numerous than the Fork-tailed. Black and Ashy Petrels nest locally off the south California coast only. The Fulmar, as on the Atlantic coasts, nests on open cliffs in the far North. Many other so-called 'tubenoses' can be seen off the coast, but as they are visiting birds they will be described at the end of the chapter.

Four species of cormorant inhabit the west coast. The Double-crested Cormorant is already familiar from other parts of the continent. It finds nesting grounds along the entire coast. The Red-faced Cormorant, on the other hand, is limited to the Bering Sea region where it often nests in association with the various alcids of this area. Brandt's Cormorant is limited to the southern half of the coast. The Pelagic Cormorant, nesting from the Aleutians to northern California, places its nest on steep and inaccessible ledges, whereas the others prefer the boulders or flatter rocks near the water's edge. The Pelagic Cormorant also seems to be able to dive deeper than most other cormorants, thus limiting interspecific competition for food.

Even more numerous than the cormorants in the seabird colonies are the many alcids found in the North Pacific, some of which have already been mentioned in chapter three. It seems that during the glacial periods the Bering Sea region was an isolated area in which rich opportunities for the development of new species, particularly within this group, existed.

As on the Atlantic coast, the Thick-billed Murre or Brünnich's Guillemot, which inhabits the ledges of steep cliffs in the arctic is replaced further south by the Common Murre or Guillemot. On the Pacific the Pigeon Guillemot is the counterpart of the Black Guillemot of the Atlantic. Similarly the Horned Puffin replaces the Common Puffin. The Tufted Puffin, too, can be found nesting as far south as islands off the California coast.

In addition to these species there are a confusing number of smaller alcids. Cassin's and Rhinoceros Auklets share their hole-nesting and nocturnal habits with the Ancient Murrelets. Kittlitz's Murrelet lays its egg in the high mountains above the tree line in Alaska, a habit possibly also followed by the Marbled Murrelet, one of the least known North American birds. The Least Auklet, probably the most numerous of all the Pacific alcids in the Aleutians, shares rock crevices and even bare rocks with the much less numerous Crested and Parakeet Auklets. To the far south Xantus' Murrelet, which resembles a miniature murre, can be found; it is nocturnal in its nesting habits.

The nesting colonies of the Black-legged Kittiwakes in the north and the Glaucous-winged Gulls further south are often found close to these seabird colonies. Other gulls commonly nesting on the west coast are the Western Gull, a slightly smaller edition of the Great Black-backed Gull, and the Herring Gull. In the south the very dark-colored Heermann's Gull may visit the California coast from its more southern breeding grounds. Along the south of the Pacific coast Brown Pelicans may be found nesting in colonies in bushes or on rocks on sheltered islands. Seabird colonies often suffer greatly from disturbance by man, which in this area is becoming particularly common because of the spread of the motorboat. If the birds are scared away from the nest, gulls as well as marauding Western Crows make short work of the unprotected eggs and young. Disturbance during the breeding season should therefore be kept to an absolute minimum.

Besides the colony-nesting birds a few other species also find the rocky shores suitable for breeding, the Black Oystercatcher, for instance, an all-black edition of the black and white Oystercatcher of the sandy eastern beaches. In winter, however, several shorebirds such as Surfbird, Black Turnstone, Wandering Tattler and Rock Sandpiper—the western equivalent of the Purple Sandpiper of the Atlantic shores—can be seen exploring the rocks at the water's edge. All these birds are found breeding further north in Alaska.

The Surfbird nests in the mountains. It is unusual among birds in that it is the male Surfbird which cares for the young until they are able to undertake the journey to the shore. The Wandering Tattler is also found nesting in these mountains. This species, however, nests along mountain streams. In winter it is not only found on the west coast but scattered

throughout the many islands of the enormous Pacific Ocean. The Black Turnstone usually nests near ponds or near the coast in the far north, the Rock Sandpiper on the tundra. Snowy or Kentish Plovers and Least Terns nest along the sandy beaches. During migration a larger number of different shorebirds which nest further north may be seen. To some degree these are the same species found on the east coast. The following are a mere few of the species which can be seen on the west coast: Black-bellied or Gray Plover, Long-billed Curlew, Knot and other sandpipers, Sanderling and Long-billed Dowitcher.

Although not found on the west coast, the amazing travels of the Bristle-thighed Curlew deserves mention. This species nests in the Alaskan mountains. Each fall this shorebird sets off on a 6,000 mile non-stop journey to its wintering grounds in Hawaii, only to reverse this journey in the spring.

A few miles offshore are the visiting pelagic birds. Besides the petrels and the Fulmar already mentioned which are indigenous to North America, Pacific species such as the Black-footed and Laysan Albatrosses may be seen. Different shearwaters may also be encountered such as the Pink-footed and the abundant Sooty Shearwaters from the Southern Hemisphere, for instance. Many of the alcids feed out of sight of land so it is thus well worth taking a short boat trip off the shore and venturing into the surprisingly rich life of the open sea which, in spite of pollution with oil and poisoning by insecticides, has still suffered less from the destruction of man than the landmass of North America.

Two variants of the Common Murre are shown here. The 'ringed' phase is the rarer

Far left The Glaucous-winged Gull is very common along the west coast

Left Brandt's Cormorant nests colonially on the rocky shores of the Pacific

Below Double-crested Cormorants are found throughout most of North America. At favorable fishing grounds they congregate in flocks

Birds
in the City

The urbanization of North America, which has accelerated so rapidly in the past century, has created a new environment for birds as well as for man.

As long as towns and villages were small and scattered they blended to a large degree into their surroundings. Their birdlife was mainly that of the adjacent areas, whether fields, woods, mountains, deserts or prairies. Although certain species might be more attracted to such a modified 'landscape' than others, no really new landscape on a large scale was created. Today, however, with cities and suburbs sprawling over hundreds of square miles, a new and important environment has been created with conditions very different from those prevailing in the surrounding areas.

Long before North America was settled several birds in the Old World had associated themselves with man and his dwellings. Probably the first to do so was the House Sparrow which took advantage of the nesting sites offered in the many crevices of houses and huts and the relatively abundant food supply provided by agriculture. However, like man, House Sparrows gradually adapted themselves to a more urban existence and remained with man as his cities grew. Nevertheless, rather densely settled farmland still offers the greatest concentration of this species.

House Sparrows were first introduced into North America in about 1850 when several pairs were let loose in New York and other eastern cities. The bird was soon well established in the east and a rapid westward expansion began. This was partly accomplished with the help of man in transporting the birds deliberately or accidentally, in railroad cars for example. Shortly after the turn of the century the House Sparrow covered almost the entire cultivated and more densely inhabited parts of North America. House Sparrows are now so closely associated with

man that the species probably would not be able to survive alone. The Tree Sparrow, which in parts of Asia fills the same ecological niche as the House Sparrow, was introduced to St Louis in 1870. At first it did well, but when the House Sparrow extended its range, the Tree Sparrow was forced out of the inner city into the surrounding more rural districts. Remnants of this Tree Sparrow population still exist.

The Starling is another example of a bird which, although more loosely associated with man than the House Sparrow, has greatly benefited from his new environment. It was first introduced into Central Park in New York in 1890 and was well established in the entire New York area twenty years later. From here it spread rapidly and today, like the House

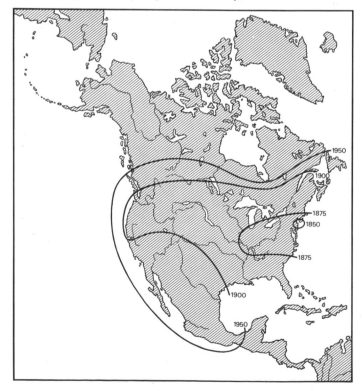

Sparrow, inhabits almost the entire continent. Characteristic of the Starling are the enormous flocks in which it occurs outside the breeding season. In the countryside these flocks roost in reedbeds, often together with Redwings and Grackles, but in cities in unmixed flocks under bridges and in viaducts. These night roosts can contain hundreds of thousands of birds and a congregation of the smaller flocks at nightfall is one of the most spectacular birdwatching experiences in the city. In the early morning, when smaller flocks of Starlings leave their roosts, they can be seen as successive rings on radar, so-called 'ring angels'.

Probably as old as the association of man and House Sparrow is his relationship with the Feral Pigeon. The wild 'non-urbanized' ancestor of the Feral Pigeon, the Rock Dove, still exists in some European mountains. Like the House Sparrow, the Rock Dove took advantage of the nesting sites and food offered by man's agricultural activities. Whereas the food supply probably is the greatest attraction of man to the House Sparrow, it seems more likely that the nesting and roosting sites offered by buildings have been the main lure for the pigeon. The pigeon, however, also offered man advantages as it is sufficiently large and tasty to be worthwhile killing for food. Rock Doves were domesticated, but in such a way that a free life was pursued by the majority of the population. As cities took their present form they offered increasing advantages to the pigeons. Skyscrapers are inundated with high niches and ledges where the pigeon is safe from any intruder. The food supply is large, mainly in the form

of bread and other tidbits, so it is little wonder that the Feral Pigeon has become a characteristic bird of all our cities. Unfortunately, pigeons are carriers of certain fungal diseases affecting man and in many cities attempts to limit the populations have been made; extermination policies, however, have by and large been unsuccessful.

Feral Pigeons have few enemies which could control their numbers. Peregrine Falcons take a few and occasionally used to be found near cities in which the ever-present pigeons were established. Partly because of the shyness of the predator, but mainly because of the recent catastrophic decline in numbers previously described, even this danger for the pigeons has disappeared.

Several other foreign birds have been introduced in various towns and suburbs but none has been as successful as the House Sparrow, Starling and Pigeon. This is the case of such species as Spotted Dove and Ringed Turtle Dove, Red-whiskered Bulbul and Crested Mynah. They remain local curiosities without great impact beyond one or two city limits.

Besides the introduced species, the new ecological zone of the city has become inhabited by other birds which have been able to accommodate themselves to the changing world. The hundreds of tons of garbage disposed of daily have offered a unique food supply for gulls, Herring Gulls in particular. Their numbers have soared in the past few decades and other gulls, like the Greater Black-backed, Western, Bonaparte's, Mew and Ring-billed Gulls, often rely heavily on the food offered in harbors and on the garbage dumps of the great cities. Common Crows share the garbage dumps with the gulls and both Black and Turkey Vultures are common in southern cities.

Surrounding the concrete desert of the inner city are the suburbs with their many lawns, bushes, flowers and fruit trees. This landscape has benefited several species. Robins find an abundance of food as do grackles, Catbirds, Chickadees, Cardinals and Mourning Doves. Blue Jays abound. In the south Mockingbirds use television aerials for song posts and in the south-west several hummingbirds are attracted by the many flowers of the gardens. The Purple Finch in the east and, even more so, the House Finch in the west, are very common in many suburban areas, and are now probably far more numerous than they were prior to the arrival of man.

Many hole-nesting species have suffered from the lack of old and dead trees in this habitat, but many are easily enticed to nest in artificial nestboxes of various types. This is true of Great Crested Flycatchers, Phoebes, Chickadees, House Wrens and

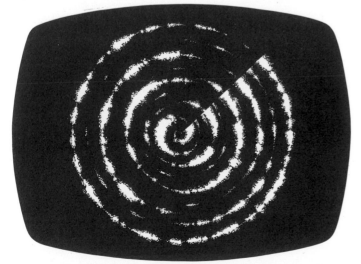

Left The spread of the House Sparrow through North America after its introduction to New York in 1850

Above 'Ring angel', flocks of Starlings dispersing at dawn from a central roost as they can be seen on radar

Top opposite Probably the North American species most adaptable to human habitation has been the House Finch. Originally western in distribution it is now spreading in the east

Bottom opposite The Mockingbird, with its preference for park-like habitats, has readily adopted the suburban landscape

Left The Starling, introduced about 100 years ago, has become a pest in many areas

Below The Tree Sparrow has been one of the less successfully introduced species; remnants of the original population exist today in the St Louis area

Bluebirds. Even Sparrow Hawks can be enticed to nest in a box. Purple Martins are social nesters and in many areas are totally dependent on man-made nestboxes for breeding. Even before the arrival of the white man Indians attracted Purple Martins by hanging up gourds for nestboxes.

Nestboxes are not only important for the breeding of many species; in winter the boxes are used by different kinds of birds for sleeping quarters.

In city areas birds are fed at feeding stations when their natural food supply is no longer available, making it possible for species like Robins and Catbirds to survive the winter much further north than would be possible without the aid of man.

Large cities also offer very special ecological niches: sewage farms where shorebirds can congregate; the large grass flats of airports where Sparrow Hawks and Burrowing Owls sometimes join the Cowbirds, Starlings, Redwings and other species, and finally zoos where, for instance, the large number of rats and mice give food for Black-crowned Night Herons and owls.

Feeding stations such as this make it possible for some species to remain further north than normal in winter; on the left two Oregon Juncos, on the right a Song Sparrow

Several cities have major bird sanctuaries within their limits—Jamaica Bay in New York, for example—which give large numbers of the urban population the chance of seeing wildlife at close quarters. Other towns have been declared sanctuaries in themselves as, for instance, Cape May in New Jersey.

Many cities lie on the major migration routes. The city parks are veritable oases for these traveling birds which would otherwise find themselves in a dismal desert of bricks and concrete. At times of migration, in fall and spring, many city parks are therefore alive with birds of various kinds. At this time the city-dwelling birdwatcher may see a large variety of species whose breeding grounds he otherwise might have to travel hundreds of miles to find.

The city is not devoid of birds, but is a new kind of habitat strangly ignored by the birdlover, but not by the birds. Much more could be done to conserve and enrich the birdlife of our cities, to give the birds a chance to adapt to the most extreme change man has wrought upon the environment, the creation of the far-flung city.

Map of the ecological zones of North America

Arctic-Alpine	Pacific Rain Forest	Mesquite-Grassland
Open Boreal	East. Deciduous Forest	Pinyon-Juniper
Closed Boreal	Grasslands	Chaparral-Oak Woodland
No. Hardwood-Conifer	Oak-Savannah	Southern Evergreen
Aspen Parkland	Northern Desert Scrub	Mexican Pine and Pine-Oak
Montane Woodland	Southern Desert Scrub	Tropical Areas (combined)

Bibliography

American Ornithologists' Union, *Checklist of North American Birds*, 5th ed. American Ornithologists' Union, Baltimore, Md., 1957.

Austin, Oliver L., Jr, *Birds of the World*. Golden Press, New York, 1961.

Bent, Arthur Cleveland, *Life Histories of North American Birds*, 20 vols. U.S. Nat. Mus., Washington, D.C., 1919–1968 (reprinted by Dover).

Fisher, James and Peterson, Roger Tory, *The World of Birds*. Doubleday, Garden City, N.Y., 1964.

Godfrey, W. Earl, *The Birds of Canada*. National Museum of Canada, Ottawa, 1966.

Griscom, Ludlow and Sprunt, Alexander, Jr, *The Warblers of North America.* Devin-Adain, New York, 1957.

Kortright, Francis H., *The Ducks, Geese and Swans of North America.* Wildlife Mgmt. Inst., Washington, D.C., 1953.

Matthiessen, Peter, *The Shorebirds of North America*. Viking, New York, 1967.

Palmer, Ralph S. (Ed.), *Handbook of North American Birds*. Vol. 1, *Loons Through Flamingos*. Yale University Press, New Haven, 1962.

Peterson, Roger Tory, *A Field Guide to the Birds*, 1947; *A Field Guide to the Birds of Texas and Adjacent States*, 1963; *A Field Guide to Western Birds*, 1961; all Houghton Mifflin, Boston.

Pettingill, Olin Sewall, Jr, *A Guide to Bird-Finding East of the Mississippi*, 1951; *A Guide to Bird-Finding West of the Mississippi*, 1953; both Oxford University Press, New York. Editor, *The Bird Watcher's America*. McGraw-Hill, New York, 1965.

Pough, Richard H., *Audubon Land Bird Guide*, 1949; *Audubon Water Bird Guide*, 1951; *Audubon Western Bird Guide*, 1957; all Doubleday, Garden City, N.Y.

Robbins, Chandler S., Bruun, Bertel and Zim, Herbert, *Birds of North America*. Golden Press, New York, 1966.

Sanderson, Ivan T., *The Continent We Live On*. Random House, New York, 1961.

Saunders, Aretas A., *A Guide to Bird Songs*. Doubleday, New York, 1959.

Sprunt, Alexander, Jr, *North American Birds of Prey*. Harper and Bros, New York, 1955.

Wetmore, Alexander and others. *Song and Garden Birds of North America; Water, Prey and Game Birds of North America*. National Geographic Society, Washington, D.C. 1964–65.

Index

Page numbers in italic refer to illustrations